Insider's Guide to Teaching with Excursions in Modern Mathematics

Seventh Edition

Peter Tannenbaum
California State University—Fresno

Prentice Hall
is an imprint of

Executive Editor	Anne Kelly
Acquisitions Editor	Marnie Greenhut
Senior Managing Editor	Karen Wernholm
Project Manager	Elizabeth Bernardi
Developmental Editor	Abby Tanenbaum
Assistant Editor	Leah Goldberg
Editorial Assistant	Leah Driska
Digital Assets Manager	Marianne Groth
Production Coordinator	Katherine Roz
Composition	Suzanne Roark
Executive Marketing Manager	Becky Anderson
Marketing Assistant	Katherine Minton

The author and publisher of this book have used their best efforts in preparing this book. These efforts include the development, research, and testing of the theories and programs to determine their effectiveness. The author and publisher make no warranty of any kind, expressed or implied, with regard to these programs or the documentation contained in this book. The author and publisher shall not be liable in any event for incidental or consequential damages in connection with, or arising out of, the furnishing, performance, or use of these programs.

Reproduced by Pearson Prentice Hall from QuarkXPress® files.

ISBN-10: 0-321-57620-9
ISBN-13: 978-0-321-57620-0

3 4 5 6 OPM 12 11 10 09

Prentice Hall
is an imprint of

www.pearsonhighered.com

CONTENTS

INTRODUCTION

Dear Faculty:

The Tannenbaum book team at Pearson is very excited that you will be using *Excursions in Modern Mathematics*, Seventh Edition. We know that whether you are teaching this course for the first time or the tenth time, you will face many challenges, including how to prepare for class, how to make the most effective use of your class time, how to present the material to your students in a manner that will make sense to them, how best to assess your students, and the list goes on.

This manual is designed to make your job easier. Inside these pages are words of advice from experienced instructors, general and content-specific teaching tips, tips on using both student and instructor supplements that accompany this text, and a professional bibliography provided by your fellow instructors.

We would like to thank the following professors for sharing their advice and teaching tips. This manual would not be what it is without their valuable contributions.

MaryAnne Anthony, *Santa Ana College*

Molly L. Beauchman, *Yavapai College*

Norma Biscula, *University of Maine, Augusta*

Kevin Chouinard, *Northern Virginia Community College*

Rosemary Danaher, *Sacred Heart University*

Robert V. DeLiberato, *Saint Joseph's University*

Olivia Garcia, *The University of Texas at Brownsville and Texas Southmost College*

Alicia Gordon, *Meredith College*

Julie March, *Onondaga Community College, SUNY*

Margaret Michener, *University of Nebraska at Kearney*

Margaret Morrow, *SUNY Plattsburgh*

Tejinder S. Neelon, *California State University San Marcos*

Kathleen Offenholley, *Brookdale Community College*

LaRonda Oxendine, *Robeson Community College*

Linda Padilla, *Joliet Junior College*

Ryan Sieve, *University of Kansas*

Deirdre Smith, *University of Arizona*

Debra Wood, *University of Arizona*

It is also important to know that you have a very valuable resource available to you in your Pearson sales representative. If you do not know your representative, you can locate him/her by logging on to www.pearsonhighered./replocator and typing in the zip code of your institution. Please feel free to contact your representative if you have any questions relating to our text or if you need additional supplements. Of course, you can always contact us directly at math@pearson.com.

We know that teaching this course can be challenging. We hope that this and the other resources we have provided will help to minimize the amount of time it takes you to meet those challenges.

Good luck in your endeavors!

The Tannenbaum book team

GETTING STARTED

1 How to Be an Effective Teacher

(From David Royse, *Teaching Tips for College and University Instructors: A Practical Guide*, published by Allyn & Bacon, Boston, MA. © 2001 by Pearson Education, Inc.. Adapted by permission of the publisher.)

A look at fifty years of research "on the way teachers teach and learners learn" reveals five broad principles of good teaching practice (Chickering and Gamson, 1987).

Five Principles of Good Teaching Practice

1. **Frequent student-faculty contact:** Faculty who are concerned about their students and their progress and who are perceived to be easy to talk to, serve to motivate and keep students involved.

   Things you can do to apply this principle:

   - Attend events sponsored by students.
   - Serve as a mentor or advisor to students.
   - Keep "open" or "drop-in" office hours.

2. **The encouragement of cooperation among students:** There is a wealth of research indicating that students benefit from the use of small-group and peer-learning instructional approaches.

   Things you can do to apply this principle:

   - Have students share in class their interests and backgrounds.
   - Create small groups to work on projects together.
   - Encourage students to study together.

3. **Prompt feedback:** Learning theory research has consistently shown that the quicker the feedback, the greater the learning.

   Things you can do to apply this principle:

   - Return quizzes and exams by the next class meeting.
   - Return homework within one week.
   - Provide students with detailed comments on their written papers.

4. **Emphasize time on task:** This principle refers to the amount of actual involvement with the material being studied and applies, obviously, to the way the instructor uses classroom instructional time. Faculty need good time-management skills.

   Things you can do to apply this principle:

   - Require students who miss classes to make up lost work.
   - Require students to rehearse before making oral presentations.
   - Don't let class breaks stretch out too long.

5. **Communicating high expectations:** The key here is not to make the course impossibly difficult but to have goals that can be attained as long as individual learners stretch and work hard, going beyond what they already know.

   Things you can do to apply this principle:

   - Communicate your expectations orally and in writing at the beginning of the course.
   - Explain the penalties for students who turn work in late.
   - Identify excellent work by students; display exemplars if possible.

2   Planning Your Course

(From David Royse, *Teaching Tips for College and University Instructors: A Practical Guide*, published by Allyn & Bacon, Boston, MA. © 2001 by Pearson Education, Inc.. Adapted by permission of the publisher.)

Constructing the syllabus: The syllabus should clearly communicate course objectives, assignments, required readings, and grading policies. Think of the syllabus as a stand-alone document. Those students who miss the first or second meeting of a class should be able to learn most of what they need to know about the requirements of the course from reading the syllabus. Start by collecting syllabi from colleagues who have recently taught the course you will be teaching and look for common threads and themes.

Problems to avoid: One mistake commonly made by educators teaching a course for the first time is that they may have rich and intricate visions of how they want students to demonstrate comprehension and synthesis of the material, but they somehow fail to convey this information to those enrolled. Check your syllabus to make sure your expectations have been fully articulated. Be very specific. Avoid vaguely worded instructions that can be misinterpreted.

3   Your First Class

(From Richard E. Lyons, Marcella L. Kysilka, & George E. Pawlas, *The Adjunct Professor's Guide to Success: Surviving and Thriving In The Classroom*, published by Allyn & Bacon, Boston, MA. © 1999 by Pearson Education, Inc.. Adapted by permission of the publisher.)

Success in achieving a great start is almost always directly attributable to the quality and quantity of planning that has been invested by the course professor. If the first meeting of your class is to be successful, you should strive to achieve seven distinct goals.

Seven Goals for a Successful First Meeting

1. **Create a positive first impression:** Renowned communications consultant Roger Ailes claims you have fewer than 10 seconds to create a positive image of yourself. Students are greatly influenced by the visual component; therefore, you must look the part of the professional professor. Dress as you would for a professional job interview. Greet each student entering the room. Be approachable and genuine.

2. **Introduce yourself effectively:** Communicate to students who you are and why you are credible as the teacher of the course. Seek to establish your approachability by "building common ground," such as stating your understanding of students' hectic lifestyles or their common preconceptions toward the subject matter.

3. **Clarify the goals and expectations:** Make a transparency of each page of the syllabus for display on an overhead projector and using a cover sheet, expose each section as you explain it. Provide clarification and elicit questions.

4. **Conduct an activity that introduces students to each other:** Students' chances of being able to complete a course effectively is enhanced if each comes to perceive the classmates as a "support network." The small amount of time you invest in an icebreaker will help create a positive classroom atmosphere and pay additional dividends throughout the term.

5. **Learn students' names:** A student who is regularly addressed by name feels more valued, is invested more effectively in classroom discussion, and will approach the professor with questions and concerns.

6. **Whet students' appetite for the course material:** The textbook adopted for the course is critical to your success. Your first meeting should include a review of its approach, features, and sequencing. Explain to students what percentage of class tests will be derived from material from the textbook.

7. **Reassure students of the value of the course:** At the close of your first meeting reassure students that the course will be a valuable learning experience and a wise investment of their time. Review the reasons why the course is a good investment: important and relevant content, interesting classmates, and a dynamic classroom environment.

4 Strategies for Teaching and Learning

(From David Royse, *Teaching Tips for College and University Instructors: A Practical Guide*, published by Allyn & Bacon, Boston, MA. © 2001 by Pearson Education, Inc.. Adapted by permission of the publisher.)

Team learning: The essential features of this small group learning approach, developed originally for use in large college classrooms are (1) relatively permanent heterogeneous task groups; (2) grading based on a combination of individual performance, group performance, and peer evaluation; (3) organization of the course so that the majority of class time is spent on small group activities; (4) a six-step instructional process similar to the following model:

1. Individual study of material outside of the class is assigned.
2. Individual testing is used (multiple-choice questions over homework at the beginning of class).
3. Groups discuss their answers and then are given a group test of the same items. They then get immediate feedback (answers).
4. Groups may prepare written appeals of items.
5. Feedback is given from instructor.
6. An application-oriented activity is assigned (e.g., a problem to be solved requiring input from all group members).

If you plan to use team learning in your class, inform students at the beginning of the course of your intentions to do so and explain the benefits of small group learning. Foster group cohesion by sitting groups together and letting them choose "identities" such as a team name or slogan. You will need to structure and supervise the groups and ensure that the projects build on newly acquired learning. Make the projects realistic and interesting and ensure that they are adequately structured so that each member's contribution is 25 percent. Students should be given criteria by which they can assess and evaluate the contributions of their peers on a project-by-project basis (Michaelson, 1994).

Tips for Thriving:

Active Learning and Lecturing

Lecturing is one of the most time-honored teaching methods, but does it have a place in an active learning environment? There are times when lecturing can be effective. Think about the following when planning a lecture:

Build interest: Capture your students' attention by leading off with an anecdote or cartoon.
Maximize understanding and retention: Use brief handouts and demonstrations as a visual backup to enable your students to see as well as hear.
Involve students during the lecture: Interrupt the lecture occasionally to challenge students to answer spot quiz questions.
Reinforce the lecture: Give students a self-scoring review test at the end of the lecture.

5   Grading and Assessment Techniques

(From Philip C. Wankat, *The Effective, Efficient Professor: Teaching Scholarship And Service,* published by Allyn & Bacon, Boston, M. © 2002 by Pearson Education, Inc.. Adapted by permission of the publisher.)

Philosophy of grading: Develop your own philosophy of grading by picturing in your mind the performance of typical A students, B students and so on. Try different grading methods until you find one that fits your philosophy and is reasonably fair. Always look closely at students on grade borders—take into account personal factors if the group is small. Be consistent with or slightly more generous than the procedure outlined in your syllabus.

Criterion grading: Professor Philip Wankat writes: "I currently use a form of criterion grading for my sophomore and junior courses. I list the scores in the syllabus that will guarantee the students A's, B's, and so forth. For example, a score of 85 to 100 guarantees an A; 75 to 85, a B; 65 to 75, a C; and 55 to 65, a D. If half the class gets above 85% they all get an A. This reduces competition and allows students to work together and help each other. The standard grade gives students something to aim for and tells them exactly what their grade is at any time. For students whose net scores are close to the borders at the end of the course, I look at other factors before deciding a final grade such as attendance."

✔ **Tips for Thriving:**

Result Feedback

As stated earlier, feedback on results is the most effective of motivating factors. Anxious students are especially hungry for positive feedback. You can quickly and easily provide it by simply writing "Great job!" on the answer sheets or tests. For students who didn't perform well, a brief note such as "I'd love to talk with you at the end of class" can be especially reassuring. The key is to be proactive and maintain high standards, while requiring students to retain ownership of their success.

(From Philip C. Wankat, *The Effective, Efficient Professor: Teachin, Scholarship And Service,* published by Allyn & Bacon, Boston, MA. © 2002 by Pearson Education, Inc.. Adapted by permission of the publisher.)

Cheating: Cheating is one behavior that should not be tolerated. Tolerating cheating tends to make it worse. Prevention of cheating is much more effective than trying to cure it once it has occurred. A professor can prevent cheating by:

- Creating rapport with students
- Gaining a reputation for giving fair tests
- Giving clear instructions and guidelines before, during, and after tests
- Educating students on the ethics of plagiarism
- Requiring periodic progress reports and outlines before a paper is due

Try to develop exams that are perceived as fair and secure by students. Often, the accusation that certain questions were tricky is valid as it relates to ambiguous language and trivial material. Ask your mentor or an experienced instructor to closely review the final draft of your first few exams for these factors.

(From David Royse, *Teaching Tips for College and University Instructors: A Practical Guide,* published by Allyn & Bacon, Boston, MA. © 2001 by Pearson Education, Inc.. Adapted by permission of the publisher.)

Unmotivated students: There are numerous reasons why students may not be motivated. The "required course" scenario is a likely explanation—although politics in colonial America is your life's work, it is safe to assume that not everyone will share your enthusiasm. There are also personal reasons such as a death of a loved one or depression. Whenever you detect a pattern that you assume to be due to lack of motivation (e.g., missing classes, not handing assignments in on time, nonparticipation in class), arrange a time to have the student meet with you outside the classroom. Candidly express your concerns and then listen.

✔ Tips for Thriving:

Discipline

One effective method for dealing with some discipline problems is to ask the class for feedback (Angelo & Cross, 1993) In a one-minute quiz, ask the students, "What can I do to help you learn?" Collate the responses and present them to the class. If behavior such as excessive talking appears in some responses (e.g., "Tell people to shut up") this gives you the backing to ask students to be quiet. Use of properly channeled peer pressure is often effective in controlling undesired behavior.

Motivating students is part of the faculty members' job. To increase motivation, professors should show enthusiasm for the topic, use various media and methods to present material, use humor in the classroom, employ activities that encourage active learning, and give frequent, positive feedback.

(From Sharon Baiocco, Jamie N. De Waters, *Successful College Teaching: Problem Solving Strategies of Distinguished Professors,* published by Allyn & Bacon, Boston, MA. © 1998 by Pearson Education, Inc.. Adapted by permission of the publisher.)

Credibility problems: If you are an inexperienced instructor, you may have problems with students not taking you seriously. At the first class meeting, articulate clear rules of classroom decorum and conduct yourself with dignity and respect for students. Try to exude that you are in charge and are the "authority" and avoid trying to pose as the students' friend.

(From Richard E. Lyons, Marcella L. Kysilka & George E. Pawlas, *The Adjunct Professor's Guide to Success: Surviving and Thriving In The Classroom,* published by Allyn & Bacon, Boston, MA. © 1999 by Pearson Education, Inc.. Adapted by permission of the publisher.)

Self-evaluation: The instructor who regularly engages in systematic self-evaluation will unquestionably derive greater reward from the formal methods of evaluation commonly employed by colleges and universities. One method for providing structure to an ongoing system of self-evaluation is to keep a journal of reflections on your teaching experiences. Regularly invest 15 or 20 introspective minutes following each class meeting to focus especially on the strategies and events in class that you feel could be improved. Committing your thoughts and emotions enables you to develop more effective habits, build confidence in your teaching performance, and make more effective comparisons later. The following questions will help guide self-assessment:

> *How do I typically begin a class?*
> *Where/How do I position myself in the class?*
> *How do I move in the classroom?*
> *Where are my eyes usually focused?*
> *Do I facilitate students' visual processing of course material?*
> *Do I change the speed, volume, energy, and tone of my voice?*
> *How do I ask questions of students?*
> *How often, and when, do I smile or laugh in class?*
> *How do I react when students are inattentive?*
> *How do I react when students disagree or challenge what I say?*
> *How do I typically end a class?*

✔ Tips for Thriving:

Video-Recording Your Class

In recent years, a wide range of professionals has markedly improved their job performance by employing video recorders in their preparation efforts. As an instructor, an effective method might be to ask your mentor or another colleague to tape a 10- to 15-minute mini-lesson, then to debrief it using the assessment questions above. Critiquing a videotaped session provides objectivity and is therefore more likely to effect change. Involving a colleague as an informal coach will enable you to gain from their experience and perspective and will reduce the chances of your engaging in self-depreciation.

References

Ailes, R. (1996) *You are the message: Getting what you want by being who you are.* New York: Doubleday.

Chickering, A. W., & Gamson, Z. F. (1987) "Seven principles for good practice in undergraduate education." *AAHE Bulletin,* 39, 3–7.

Michaelson, L. K. (1994). Team Learning: Making a case for the small-group option. In K. W. Prichard & R. M. Sawyer (Eds.), *Handbook of college teaching.* Westport, CT: Greenwood Press.

Sorcinelli, M. D. (1991). Research findings on the seven principles. In A.W. Chickering & Z. Gamson (eds.), "Applying the seven principles of good practice in undergraduate education." *New Directions for Teaching and Learning* 47. San Francisco: Jossey-Bass.

General Teaching Advice

We asked the contributing professors for words of advice to instructors who are teaching this course. Their responses can be found on the following pages.

Robert V. DeLiberato, *Saint Joseph's University*

1. Get students involved in creating their own examples of the material that is being presented in the course. Constructing their own examples gets them more actively engaged in the learning process. Evaluating the examples offered by students helps diagnose conceptual or fundamental deficiencies being encountered in the material. Students are less likely to read the textbook as required reading than they are to use it as reference material to create their own examples.

2. There is always a balancing act involved in reviewing fundamental concepts that form the basis for material being taught in the course. I often teach service courses, or required courses in mathematics to freshman students majoring in business or social sciences. I have always found it to be worthwhile to check for understanding of fundamentals, and to invest the time required to reteach material that is essential to success in the course. If students do not possess the prerequisite skills, I think of it as my responsibility to teach it to them; they will not be able to succeed in the course without the foundation material. So, my general suggestion would be, "teach to the level of where your students are, as opposed to where you might have ideally hoped or presumed they might be."

3. Be open to digressions. There are times when students might have a tendency to lead the class onto nonproductive tangents, and you will need to step in and bring the class back into focus. But, in general, I find that students who participate actively tend to lead the class down interesting and productive paths that you might not have otherwise initiated. So, don't be afraid to depart from your scripted plan for the day. There are always ways to "make up time" if the divergent path is an instructive one.

4. Turn learning challenges into opportunities. Exploring a student's learning frustrations and expanding the borders of your response will often clarify issues in the minds of other students who were reticent to ask. The way you react to what you view as "basic" or "remedial" questions will determine the willingness of other students to ask questions and participate in discussions. An actively engaged class is always preferable to a lecture class.

5. Decide ahead of time that you will learn something new from your students each semester. It has happened to me with each course I have taught, and I think this is influenced by the fact that I expect it to happen, so I am actively seeking out opportunities.

6. Get students engaged and actively participating as quickly as possible. In the first few classes, it can be as simple as learning their names. Recognizing their body language and being sure to create opportunities in each class for many of them to be involved—doing problems on the board, offering ideas, asking questions, helping to shape the "lecture" part of the class.

7. Don't be afraid to ask for feedback. After the first week of classes, I ask for a "show of hands" on some basic issues—pace of the course, style of teaching, relevance of the assignments in reinforcing the material being taught. I always try to give my students three options (too fast, too slow, and just right). This only takes a minute and it provides valuable feedback. This can be supplemented with classroom assessments using one-page forms that ask for anonymous feedback in 5 to 8 key areas of instructional design. You can distribute the forms in the last two minutes of class, ask students to fill them out, and tabulate results in less than 5 minutes. Be sure to share the results of the informal and formal surveys with students and let them know what adjustments, if any, you are planning, as a result of their feedback. Their interest in providing candid feedback is directly proportional to the professor's demonstration that he or she is listening and considering their suggestions. I try to gather feedback in some form at the end of weeks 1, 3, 5

and at mid-term. The key is to make the assessments short, concise, and relevant to the most important issues, and easy for you and the students to do it.

Margaret Michener, *University of Nebraska at Kearney*

1. All of the homework I collect over the semester adds up to one test grade. This encourages students to keep up with the homework, as I never tell them when I'm going to pick it up. It is also a good motivator to come to class every time since I don't accept late homework unless they have a doctor's note or it is a school-sponsored absence. The students who don't test well like homework grades because this rewards them for day-to-day work.

2. I have students do mostly odd-numbered exercises for homework, even though the answers are in the book and *Student Resource Guide*. That way, students know if they are working the exercises correctly or not. They need to show all their work for full credit. Whenever I assign even-numbered problems, I always go over the answers right away and we discuss any questions they have on homework before I start the new material. When I pick up homework for a grade, I give half credit for working a problem that is not correct, rewarding them for trying to get the correct answer.

3. Many students seem to do well when they can work with another student or two in the class and study together for a test. For this reason, I have them exchange phone numbers or e-mail addresses with a couple of others in the class on the first day we meet. This way, each has a contact person besides me for lecture notes and homework assignments when they are absent.

Margaret Morrow, *SUNY Plattsburgh*

1. Many students taking this kind of course are really afraid of mathematics and are unwilling to try to do the problems or assignments. Make the course as entertaining and lighthearted as you can.

2. When calculations or formulas occur, be ready to proceed very slowly, and to offer extra help and encouragement to the students. That said, I usually have a few students in the class who find the level of mathematics easy. Try to have extension activities available for these students.

3. Many students taking this course do not buy into the importance of keeping up with the material, and of doing the assigned homework before the next class period to succeed in the class. Try to find some way of ensuring that the students do the homework exercises when assigned.

4. Most students in this course do not read the text unless there is some pressure on them to do so. I have found that providing reading guides really helps when I specifically want the students to read material in the text.

5. I find it really effective to give students in this course writing assignments in which they reflect on the relevance of the course material to their own lives. I sometimes do this in the form of two or three papers during the semester, sometimes as weekly journal entries. I specify in the instructions for these assignments that the writing must convince me that the student sees the relevance of course material to their own lives. I believe that being made to write about the material in this way helps students to develop more positive attitudes to the material. If you decide to incorporate such writing, take care not to commit too much time to grading it! With experience, it is possible to grade this writing fairly quickly.

Ryan Sieve, *University of Kansas*

1. Be interactive: Class time should not always be lecture. Find ways to break students into groups, work on their own and check with a neighbor, or have the students become the teacher. It is very easy to zone out a professor, but peer-led teaching provides an environment conducive to learning.

2. Tell stories: The best way to convey a point during lecture, and make it stick, is to give your students a story to explain the material. While this cannot always be practical, I find that students consistently remember the stories and consequently the material that accompanies it.

3. Offer "tips and tricks": A "hidden" method to approach the problems intrigues students. Students love the idea of "insider information" on how to handle particularly difficult problems. This can also be used as motivation to improve class attendance.

4. Find ways to engage your students during lectures: Use humor, give "real-world" applications, or simply call on them to explain the material back to you. If you do not provide your students with a means to grasp the material and make it their own during class, the information will never truly be absorbed.

Deirdre Smith, University of Arizona

1. Since the audience in this class tends to be students who have had little success in mathematics in the past, I emphasize on the first day of class that this is a course that will emphasize real-world uses of mathematics. In general, this is a terminal math class for most of the students at our university (with the exception of elementary education majors). Because of this, my goal in this class is to make the course a pleasant experience for the students while teaching a few mathematical skills that they can use in their everyday lives.

2. Most of the students in this course think that math is about mindlessly manipulating symbols, like they did in algebra classes. For the most part, this never made sense to any of them. I emphasize that much of the math we will be seeing over the semester will involve little algebra (except the section we do on finance). I emphasize that this course is about topics that mostly involve simple computations. Mostly what I want them to do is understand and to be able to explain what we are doing in the sections that are taught.

3. I do a lot of group work in this class, especially when we do the material on graphs. I start the course teaching this material because I think it lends itself to group work. I like to do lots of group work in the beginning of the semester because it helps the students to get to know each other better. They seem to be more willing to talk in class in later sections because of this familiarity.

4. I think the material in this course lends itself to using student projects. I used to do two projects, but mostly due to the tremendous amount of time it took to grade these projects, I finally settled on one project. The project I use is a mock buying of a home. This is a rather extensive project that requires research throughout the semester. The students do several mini-projects that involve researching what they want to do for a living and finding the pay, setting up a budget, saving for 5 years, finding a house, and researching all the other costs of buying a home. The other project that I had the students do in the past was creating, conducting, and writing up the results of a survey. I had some wonderful results with these surveys. I told the students to think up a topic that interested them. On occasion I got stupid topics like "What is your favorite color?" but I got some great surveys that were well thought out and well executed. There are two projects that I especially remember. One was done by a Native American student who did a survey on how Native Americans felt about the controversy about using Indian names for school team names. She did her survey at a national powwow that had a huge representation of Native American tribes. The other was done by a student who lived in a community that was on the outskirts of Tucson that was being rapidly developed. She wanted to find out how long-time residents felt about this development (both the pros and cons). She randomly called a fairly large percentage of the residents and wrote a great paper on the topic. One word of warning about projects: I have found that allowing a student to do a project like a biography provides too much of a temptation for the student to cheat.

5. Do all the homework problems before you make your list of assignments. This ensures that a problem is not a lot harder than it looked and also that you do indeed cover a broad range of problems both in terms of adequately covering the material and difficulty range. This is also a good idea because you will be better able to respond to any student questions about the assignment.

6. In this class, like any math class, it is imperative that the students do the homework. I generally have an assignment due at the end of a chapter, but I emphasize repeatedly at the beginning of the semester that it takes a week (and sometimes more) to cover each chapter. I tell them that if they start the assignment the night before it is due (which they tend to do in this freshman-level course), they will be unable to finish the assignment on time. Most of them take me at my word and start the assignment immediately. Some do not and learn this lesson the hard way. Homework is always graded for correctness and the grade counts toward their final grade. (I do drop 10% off the total number of possible points before computing their average.) One suggestion for dealing with procrastinators is to break up the assignment. I have difficulty doing this because I stop at different places in the chapter each semester I teach the course, depending on student input. I find it best for me to put the responsibility on the students to keep up with the assignments with a little bit of gentle nagging in the beginning of the semester.

7. Some instructors do not grade homework for correctness; they just check to see that the work has been completed. I think this is a mistake. Grading homework takes a tremendous amount of time, but I think it is worth it. It is better that the students know immediately that they are not getting the material. If they do not get feedback, they will not know they are doing the problems wrong until they take a test,

which is obviously too late. At the end of the semester I do adjust the homework score. When students come to me and complain about being graded on the homework, I always tell them that in my years of teaching I have never seen the homework grade hurt a student's grade unless he or she did not do the homework. The homework grade tends to be consistent with the test grades, or often higher.

8. To keep the students engaged, I use a variety of teaching styles. I do some lecturing, but try not to do all the talking during the period. I also have the students do some problems in class, either alone or with a neighbor. I will then have a student walk me through the problem. Many years ago I would have a student get up and do the problem on the board, but I found that not to work well because it was hard to tell what the student was doing most of the time. I also have some group work. For certain topics I have students bring in examples and talk to the class about what they found. (This works well for Statistics.)

SAMPLE SYLLABI

Note: These syllabi refer to the Sixth Edition of *Excursions in Modern Mathematics*. Chapter, section, and exercise references may not correlate to the Seventh Edition.

Provided by:

Robert V. DeLiberato, *Saint Joseph's University*
Julie March, *Onondaga Community College, CUNY*
Margaret Morrow, *SUNY Plattsburgh*
Peter Tannenbaum, *California State University—Fresno*

Sample Course Syllabus
MAT 1171—Topics in Contemporary Mathematics

Textbook: *Excursions in Modern Mathematics* by Peter Tannenbaum, Sixth Edition, Pearson Prentice Hall, 2007.

Calculator: Basic calculator with exponential, logarithmic, and memory functions

Learning Objectives

By the end of this course, the student will be able to:

- Understand the mathematics and paradoxes associated with voting.

- Determine the outcome of an election using various methods; analyze the fairness and limitations of each election method.

- Describe and represent weighted voting systems and calculate the distribution of power in these systems.

- Compute the Banzhaf and Shapley-Shubik power indices for weighted voting systems.

- Use Euler's theorems, Fleury's algorithm, and related ideas to find efficient paths and circuits in a graph.

- Understand the traveling salesman problem, complete graphs, and Hamilton circuits.

- Apply brute-force, nearest-neighbor, and cheapest-link algorithms to find optimal and efficient Hamilton circuits.

- Create graphs of trees and minimum spanning trees and be able to explain the distinctions between circuits and trees.

- Use Kruskal's algorithm to find an optimal minimum spanning tree.

- Apply population growth models using linear and exponential functions.

Classroom and Evaluation Procedures

The learning format emphasizes problem solving through class participation, lecture and examples, and presentation of homework solutions by students in class. There will be 4 tests during the semester. Each test is worth 15% of the final semester grade. Class participation and presentation of homework solutions is worth 10% of the semester grade. There is a comprehensive final examination worth 30% of the final semester grade.

- Class attendance is essential. A student who misses a class receives a failing grade for class participation for the class missed. The student is responsible for all work associated with missed classes. A maximum of 4 absences is permitted for the semester. A student who misses 5 or more classes receives a failing grade for the course. There are no excused absences unless specifically approved by the academic dean.

- Assignments and problem sets are posted to the electronic *Blackboard* system. Students should consult this resource regularly throughout the semester.

- There are no "make-up" tests. If one test is missed for a serious illness or a documented emergency, then the student's performance on the final examination for the material covering the missed topics will count as the missed test. More than one missed test results in a failing grade for the course. Missing the final exam results in failure for the course.

- Classroom conduct: Be punctual; treat others with respect; no distracting or disruptive behavior; no "side" conversations; turn off cell phones.

- Test procedures: Calculators are permitted and required. All tests are completed in blue books distributed by the professor at the beginning of the test. No notes or note cards are permitted. No electronic devices of any kind (except for a calculator) are permitted in the room. Cell phones may not be used as calculators. Calculators may not be borrowed, so be certain that your calculator is in proper working condition in advance of each test. Students may have two calculators, in the event they want a back-up for their own use.

- Students with disabilities: Special arrangements for testing with extended time in a distraction-free environment are available for students with documented disabilities. Consult the course documents section of *Blackboard* for details regarding this issue. Arrangements must be confirmed and approval forms completed at least one week prior to the scheduled date of the test or final examination.

Grading

A (95–100)	A– (90–94)	B+ (87–89)	B (83-86)
B– (80–82)	C+ (77–79)	C (73–76)	C– (70–72)
D+ (65–69)	D (60–64)	F (59 and below)	

Academic Honesty

University policy applies. The highest standards of integrity are expected. Cheating, or assisting another student in cheating, results in failure for the course.

Onondaga Community College
Contemporary Mathematics
MAT113
Fall 2008

Instructor: Julie March

Office:

Office Hours:

Contact Information

Phone:

E-mail:

Math Department phone:

COURSE INFORMATION

Credit Hours: 3

Text: *Excursions in Modern Mathematics* by Peter Tannenbaum, 2nd custom edition for OCC

Online Practice website:

Course Description

The purpose of the course is to show the direct connection between mathematics and concrete real-life problems. The topics are drawn from the areas of social choice (voting), management science (networks and scheduling), and routing problems (graph theory). Participation in group work is required.

Prerequisite: Beginning Algebra or equivalent

COURSE CONTENT

Topics covered and Approximate Course Schedule

Management Science

Chapter 5	The Circuit Comes to Town	Euler Circuits	3.5 weeks
Chapter 6	Hamilton Joins the Circuit	Traveling Salesman	3.0 weeks
Chapter 7	It's All about Being Connected	Networks	1.5 weeks
Chapter 8	Directed Graphs and Critical Paths	Scheduling	3.0 weeks

The Mathematics of Social Choice

Chapter 1	Paradoxes of Democracy	Voting Theory	2.0 weeks
Chapter 2	The Power Game	Weighted Voting Systems	1.0 week

COURSE REQUIREMENTS

Daily Required Materials

paper or notebook, folder, writing utensil, calculator, textbook

Attendance

• Attendance is essential for success in this class.

• Any student missing 4 consecutive classes without contacting the instructor will be dropped from the class.

• Removal from this class may affect your financial aid and/or health insurance.

Class Problems

- There are approximately 15–20 class problems in this course that are collected and graded.
- Class problems are done in groups. Each group member submits a copy and every member of the group receives the same grade.
- Class problems are to be completed in class and cannot be made up.

Homework

- Homework is essential for success in this class.

Exams

- There will be 5 chapter exams.
- Exams are done individually.
- There will be no make-up exams.

Final Exam

- The final exam is cumulative and will be given during final exam week.
- The final exam is 30% of your final grade.

Final Grade

Class Problems: 30%, Exams: 40%, Final Exam: 30%

Grading Scale

A	92 and above	B	82–85	C	72–75	D	62–65
A–	89–91	B–	79–81	C–	69–71	D–	60–61
B+	86–88	C+	76–78	D+	66–68	F	Below 60

AVAILABLE SERVICES

Student Support Services

- Students may obtain help from the instructor during the above listed office hours. If you cannot make it during these times, please see me to schedule an appointment
- Students may obtain walk-in help and tutoring sessions in the Math Lab.
- Students may use the online website which can be accessed from OCC or from home.

Students with Special Needs

The Office of Services for Students with Special Needs (OSSSN) at Onondaga Community College is available to assist students who have a documented disability. If you require special accommodations for this class, visit or call the OSSSN. In addition, please see me to discuss your individual circumstances concerning this course.

MAT 133: Mathematics in Context: Spring 2008

Instructor: Dr. Margaret Morrow

Office: **Phone:**   **e-mail:**

Office Hours:

Learning Center

There will be help available in the Learning Center. Details will be provided later.

Course Description

From the catalogue: "An introductory level course for non-science majors, focusing on simple mathematical models in contexts of general interest. The course emphasizes the use of mathematics to analyze issues of interest to an informed member of society. There is emphasis on active learning. Students should expect to read and write about the applications of the mathematics, and to solve non-routine problems in the mathematics."

In this course we will explore ways of describing and analyzing the world through the lens of mathematics. (A mathematical model is simply a piece of mathematics that describes some aspect of reality.) We will explore how mathematics can provide a different perspective, and help us to think critically about issues of interest to an informed member of society. We will explore mathematics that relates to themes including elections, probability, art, and nature.

Prerequisite

Mathematics placement, or MAT 101

Required Materials

1. Text: Peter Tannenbaum, *Excursions in Modern Mathematics with Mini-Excursions,* Sixth Edition, Pearson Prentice Hall (2007).
2. Calculator: any kind as long as it is at least a scientific calculator (must have a LOG button).
3. Supplementary notes and exercises that will be provided from time to time.

Technology

We will do some work with Microsoft *Excel* (a spreadsheet program), and you will need access to a computer with *Excel* to complete assignments. You also need Internet access. You will sometimes need to access the Web site associated to your text, as well as our course Web site. You can of course use the computers in Feinberg open lab for all of this.

Course Objectives

1. To increase your appreciation for the relevance of mathematics in the world around you
2. To increase your appreciation for the role of mathematics in thinking critically about issues of interest to an informed member of society
3. To increase your awareness of different kinds of mathematics that are useful in analyzing the world around you
4. To develop your skill in using a variety of simple mathematical models to analyze the world around you
5. To strengthen the mathematical skills you need to successfully work with the mathematical models in the course
6. To strengthen your skills in solving nonroutine mathematical problems
7. To strengthen your skills in communicating ideas involving mathematics, both orally and in writing

Content Coverage

We will consider several topics in Parts 1 and 3 of your text, as well as selected topics from Parts 2 and 4.

Evaluation

Your final grade will be determined by your percentage out of 620 possible points, made up as follows:

2 in-class exams	$2 \times 100 = 200$ points
2 long quizzes	$2 \times 50 = 100$ points
Short quizzes (most weeks)	50 points
Final exam (cumulative)	100 points
Homework (Excel assignments, online reading quizzes)	50 points
Journal	100 points
Participation (Includes short class assignments, required activity on course Web site, and class participation. These are easy points to get if you participate fully!)	20 points
TOTAL:	620 points

There are set standards for grades; there is no "grading on the curve."

Lower cutoff points for grades are as follows:

A–: 90%   B–: 75%   C–: 60%   D–: 50%

Note: To obtain an A for the course, you must have at least a B average on the exams and quizzes, to obtain a B you must have at least a C average, and so on.

Provisional dates for exams and longer quizzes are indicated above. Mark your calendars!

Attendance policies: I expect you to attend all class meetings.

- *More than two absences from class or excessive late arrivals will lower your final grade.* If you miss a class, you are responsible for all that happens in that class (including responding to any announcements made, any work assigned, or any deadlines announced). Absence from class is not sufficient cause for any change in course policy. (If you have good reason for missing a class, it is a good idea to keep me informed.)

- Arrangements will be made for missed exams or long quizzes only in case of prior approval (hard to come by) or *documented* emergency. In any other circumstance, absence from an exam will result in a score of 0 for that exam. Note that in case of approved absence, "arrangements" will not necessarily be an exam in the same form as taken by the other students in the class. The exam dates are specified on this syllabus; please mark your calendars now.

- There are *no* make-ups on short quizzes or in-class assignments. Your lowest quiz score will be dropped to take account of unavoidable absence.

- If a journal assignment is not available when called for, you will receive a score of zero; no make-ups, and no late submissions.

- Assignments must be submitted by the date and time specified. Assignments submitted after the work has been graded will receive a score of 0.

Academic Honesty

It is expected that all students enrolled in this class support the letter and the spirit of the Academic Honesty Policy as stated in the college catalog. Please note that *copying (or any other kind of plagiarism) is completely unacceptable, and will be heavily penalized.* By all means work together on homework and assignments, *but when you write down your answers, write alone.*

Description of Course Activities

Class time will be used mostly for class discussion and for group work.

Homework will be assigned after every class period. It will consist of a variety of tasks, including:

- Homework exercises from the text, or from supplementary hand-outs. Although these will not usually be taken in for grading, it is essential that you keep up with them. Questions on quizzes and exams will be virtually identical to assigned questions.
- Completion of class assignments
- Computer assignments (using *Excel*, other computer software, or the Internet)
- Reading: Sometimes you will be asked to read material we have not discussed in class; other times you will be required to read materials that reinforce and extend ideas discussed in class. Often you will have to complete a *short reading quiz* on the course Web site based on the reading.

Note: When work is collected for grading, often only a random selection of the problems on the homework will be graded in depth, so it is important that you do all the questions carefully.

I expect that most of you will need to spend about **six hours per week** outside of class on homework and study.

Journal

Notice that your journal counts as much as an exam in this class. You must demonstrate in this journal that you are meeting the course objectives, in particular, that you increasing your appreciation for the relevance of mathematics to the world around you. You will be asked to show that you are able to relate the mathematics we discuss in the course to aspects of the world that you find significant and interesting.

Course Internet Site

I will often communicate with the class via this site, and via e-mail. It is essential that you check the course site and your e-mail regularly, so that you do not miss important messages. *Important: When you want to e-mail me, do so through the mail in our course site.* This is the only way you can be sure I will see and respond to your message in good time.

Final Comments

If you participate fully in class, and keep up with the required work, you will have no difficulty in this class. It also really helps to form study groups (even with just one other person) for working on the course material.

Enjoy the course!

SYLLABUS
MATH 45: WHAT IS MATHEMATICS?

TEXT

Tannenbaum, *Excursions in Modern Mathematics*, Sixth Edition, Pearson Prentice Hall, 2007.

COURSE OBJECTIVES

This is a survey course in which we will touch upon many concepts and ideas. In fact, modern mathematical ideas and how they are applied in the real world are the primary focus of the material covered in this course. The primary goal is to show you how mathematical ideas and theories get started and how they end up being used in a practical way, even where you least expect them.

A second important goal is to make this general education mathematics course a positive learning experience. I have made every effort to create and organize a course that you can pass and might even actually enjoy. All I ask from you is that you be diligent and responsible with your assignments and deadlines and approach the course with an open and inquisitive mind.

Student Learning Outcomes

Upon completion of this course, students will be able to:

1. Construct and interpret a preference schedule for an election.
2. Determine the outcome of an election (winner only or ranking of candidates) using the plurality, Borda count, pairwise-comparisons, and plurality-with-elimination methods.
3. Understand Arrow's four fairness criteria and identify violations thereof.
4. Understand the meaning and significance of Arrow's impossibility theorem.
5. Understand how to represent and interpret a weighted voting system.
6. Count the number of coalitions and sequential coalitions of a weighted voting system with N players.
7. Compute the Banzhaf power distribution of a small weighted voting system.
8. Compute the Shapley-Shubik power distribution of a small weighted voting system.
9. Identify the elements and assumptions in a fair-division game.
10. Recognize the difference between discrete and continuous fair-division problems.
11. Apply and understand the procedures behind each of the following fair-division methods: lone-divider, lone-chooser, sealed bids, and markers.
12. Identify the elements and assumptions behind the apportionment problem.
13. Implement each of the following apportionment methods: Hamilton, Jefferson, Adams, and Webster.
14. Understand the meaning of the quota rule, the Alabama paradox, and the population paradox.
15. Understand the meaning and significance of Balinski and Young's impossibility theorem.
16. Identify and model Euler circuit and Euler path problems.
17. Understand basic graph terminology.
18. Understand and apply Euler's theorems on paths and circuits.
19. Find an Euler path/Euler circuit using Fleury's algorithm.
20. Find an optimal Eulerization/semi-Eulerization in a graph.
21. Identify and model Hamilton circuit and Hamilton path problems.

22. Identify traveling salesman-type problems.

23. Implement each of the following algorithms: nearest-neighbor, repetitive nearest-neighbor, and cheapest-link.

24. Classify algorithms in terms of the optimal-approximate and efficient-inefficient dichotomies.

25. Identify and use graphs to model minimum network problems.

26. Know the properties of trees and minimum spanning trees.

27. Implement Kruskal's algorithm to find a minimum spanning tree.

28. Identify and use digraphs and project digraphs to model scheduling problems.

28. Understand and apply basic digraph terminology.

30. Implement the decreasing-time and critical-path algorithms for scheduling a project.

COURSE SCHEDULE

Chapter 1: *The Mathematics of Voting* (3 lectures)

Chapter 2: *Weighted Voting Systems* (3 lectures)

Test 1: Chapters 1 and 2

Chapter 3: *Fair Division* (3 lectures)

Chapter 4: *The Mathematics of Apportionment* (3 lectures)

Test 2: Chapters 3 and 4

Chapter 5: *Euler Circuits* (3 lectures)

Chapter 6: *The Traveling Salesman Problem* (3 lectures)

Test 3: Chapters 5 and 6

Chapter 7: *The Mathematics of Networks* (2 lectures)

Chapter 8: *The Mathematics of Scheduling* (3 lectures)

Chapter 10: *Financial Mathematics* (4 lectures)

Final Exam: Chapters 7, 8, and 10

HOMEWORK

There will be a total of 14 homework assignments (one per week except for the first and last weeks of the semester). Assignments are always due on midnight on the Monday of the week after the assignment was posted. Assignments are posted on *Blackboard* and can only be done on *Blackboard*. Only the ten highest scores will count towards your grade.

GRADING

- Three tests (15% each) = 45%
- Homework = 20%
- Final Exam = 20%
- Quizzes (iClicker) = 15%

A = 90% and above

B = 80%–89%

C = 70%–79%

D = 60%–69%

F = less than 60%

TEACHING TIPS CORRELATED TO TEXTBOOK SECTIONS

Following is a listing of the topics included in Excursions in Modern Mathematics, Seventh Edition, *as well as specific teaching tips provided by the contributing professors.*

Teaching Tips

Section 1.1

The visual depiction of preference ballots in Figure 1-1 is detailed and comprehensive. However, the crowded nature of the presentation seems to make students reluctant to immerse themselves in the details. I ask them to create their own preference ballots as quickly as possible. I check the Nielsen ratings for the 18–25-year-old ratings demographic, list the four most highly rated television shows, and ask each student to create his or her own preference ballot. Then, we begin to tally votes and use the example they constructed.

Transitivity is not as apparent a concept as I originally assumed it was. In fact, some students indicate that the cancellation of a particular television program would cause them to reorder their choices. Sometimes, a television program was ranked #2 on a preference ballot because the show is linked to the #1 preference. Cancellation of program #1 would lead to program #2 dropping lower on the revised ballot. Hence, transitivity does not hold as an inviolate assumption. This can be frustrating, but it can also be an opportunity to diverge onto the topic of statistical independence and conditional probabilities. In the end, consistent transitivity of ranking is needed for this chapter, but it is interesting to allow ambiguity to be introduced and tolerated, since the stage is being set for Arrow's impossibility theorem, a bit of a counterintuitive concept in and of itself.

Robert V. DeLiberato, *Saint Joseph's University*

■ ■ ■

Be sure that students understand that *majority* means "more than half of the votes." Most students believe it simply means "most votes" and need to unlearn this. It is essential that they understand the difference between a *majority* and a *plurality* before you begin discussing the various voting methods presented in this chapter.

Students need to understand that they must memorize which procedure goes with which method. Then it's just a matter of following the rules. Remind your students to take their time and double-check their work. A simple mistake early on could completely ruin the rest of a very long problem.

Alicia Gordon, *Meredith College*

■ ■ ■

Chapter 1
The Mathematics of Voting

1.1 **Preference Ballots and Preference Schedules**
   - Transitivity and Elimination of Candidates

1.2 The Plurality Method

- The Majority Criterion
- The Condorcet Criterion
- Insincere Voting

Teaching Tips

When counting the ballots in the MAS election example, I explain that when organizing the votes into a preference schedule that it doesn't matter the order of the columns in which they place the ballots, as long as they are counted correctly. Table 1-1 displays the results in the order of most to least ballots. I tell students that it's important to add up the numbers once they are put into the schedule to check that all the ballots are accounted for.

Margaret Michener, *University of Nebraska at Kearney*

■ ■ ■

I start by asking the students to fill out a preference ballot on some topic of interest to them. For example, I might ask, "Which topics would you like to discuss in class?" and give three choices: a) math and art; b) math and the elections; c) math and environmental issues. I draw up a preference schedule on the board based on their votes, and use this to introduce the basic terms (including the basic methods of counting the votes—plurality and Borda count). This approach results in the students being interested in the data under discussion.

Overall in this chapter, students are suitably surprised that the winner of an election can be affected by the method used to decide the winner. They are surprised by Arrow's impossibility theorem, and some find it hard to comprehend what it is really saying, and when they do comprehend it, they find it hard to believe.

Margaret Morrow, *SUNY Plattsburgh*

Section 1.2

An actively engaged class will quickly challenge the "fairness" of the plurality method. I found it worthwhile to encourage this type of debate. Sometimes, the majority criterion is misunderstood. The text states that the majority criterion is satisfied by the plurality method. Students may argue that Alisha has a plurality with 14 votes, but should not win because the majority criterion is not satisfied. This is an opportune time to discuss some of the fundamentals of mathematical logic. Time invested at this early stage of the course will make later concepts easier to resolve.

The Condorcet criterion is a crucial concept in the chapter and it is not easily understood. The marching band example presented in the text format is helpful for students whose learning styles relate well to reading tables. Most students comprehend more clearly when visual head-to-head comparisons are drawn on the board. There are times when I assign a homework problem involving food preferences. I create a ballot with a food, such as ice cream, as a plurality winner. Then, I assign a "phase two," where half the group is allergic to dairy foods. The last-place ranking of an otherwise appealing food seems to help make it more evident that ice cream cannot possibly win head-to-head, since half the people are forced to rank it last because they can't even eat it.

Robert V. DeLiberato, *Saint Joseph's University*

■ ■ ■

Teaching Tips

I explain the difference between *majority* and *plurality*. I wait to go over the fairness criteria until I have explained all four voting methods. It seems like the students understand the fairness criteria more easily this way, and I can also use these to go over advantages and disadvantages of each method. Students sometimes have trouble understanding the Condorcet criterion. That's why I go through the pairwise comparisons method first and say a Condorcet candidate with pairwise comparisons is like a majority candidate with the plurality method; a candidate doesn't have to be Condorcet to win with pairwise, but if he is he will automatically win.

Margaret Michener, *University of Nebraska at Kearney*

■ ■ ■

Some students have a hard time remembering that a plurality is different from a majority. Also one needs to take care with the logic in the statements of the fairness criteria. For example, for the Condorcet criterion, one should emphasize that if there is *no* Condorcet candidate, then there can not be a violation of the Condorcet criterion, even when the winner of the election is not a Condorcet candidate. One also needs to take some care with the distinction between saying that a "method violates a particular fairness criterion" (meaning that the criterion *may in principle be violated* if the winner is determined by this method) and saying that a fairness criterion *has been violated* in a particular election.

Margaret Morrow, *SUNY Plattsburgh*

■ ■ ■

Emphasize that a plurality is a "weaker" requirement than a majority.

Tejinder S. Neelon, *California State University San Marcos*

Section 1.3

The Borda count method is easy and accessible. Students seem relieved to be able to assign numbers and do some *actual* calculation. My suggestion is to use national rankings of college football teams from the polls. Students quickly relate to the fact that the polls use a variation of Borda count, and they consider polls unfair. As long as the BCS (Bowl Championship Series) system remains in place for college football, this example should be a solid one.

Robert V. DeLiberato, *Saint Joseph's University*

■ ■ ■

I work the Borda count method a little differently than the book. I always start out with last place having 0 points, next-to-last 1 point, and so on. I explain to students that these rankings remain the same as the book's ranking when they start with last place getting 1 vote and going up from there, but there is less work to do with my method since the whole bottom row always is 0 points. I always make sure to do Example 1.6 in class to show a disadvantage of Borda count occurs when someone who has a majority of first place votes can still lose by the Borda count method.

Margaret Michener, *University of Nebraska at Kearney*

■ ■ ■

1.3 The Borda Count Method

- What's Wrong with the Borda Count Method?

1.4 The Plurality-with-Elimination Method (Instant Runoff Voting)

- Applying the Plurality-with-Elimination Method
- What's Wrong with the Plurality-with-Elimination Method?

Teaching Tips

Students seem to have come across this method in various contexts. Some students find it surprisingly hard to figure out how many points to give to a first-place vote in the case of different numbers of candidates. Stress how this is done when introducing this method.

Margaret Morrow, *SUNY Plattsburgh*

■ ■ ■

With regard to understanding the fairness criteria, Exercise 20b is a great problem. Even though the majority criterion seems simple, this question shows that many students do not really understand what the criterion says. Instead of answering that the majority criterion is violated because the candidate that has a majority does not win using the Borda count method, many students will say that the majority criterion is violated because the person who won did not have a majority. This shows that they do not understand that often people win who did not have a majority, and that does not mean the majority criterion has been violated.

Deirdre Smith, *University of Arizona*

Section 1.4

Primary elections are the most relevant example for the plurality-with-elimination method. Most students relate easily to the idea that low vote totals translate into inability to raise funds and continue in the race. This example works best in a presidential election year, or the year immediately preceding it.

Robert V. DeLiberato, *Saint Joseph's University*

■ ■ ■

I always have students write down what the majority vote is when they do plurality-with-elimination, because if someone has a majority he automatically wins without having to do any elimination. Students usually need two or three examples of this method to understand it well. Stress the importance of eliminating until one candidate has the majority or ties. They don't have to show a new preference schedule each time unless they want to. They can just keep crossing out candidates with the fewest votes. Tell students to think of it as working backward, with the idea that it wouldn't be fair to let anybody win if they have fewer first place votes than other candidates.

Margaret Michener, *University of Nebraska at Kearney*

■ ■ ■

I do not actually rewrite the tables for this method, except the very first time I present it. Students seem to cope with this simply crossing out the candidate eliminated in each round. Emphasize the real-world applications of instant runoff voting. (This method is used in elections for political office in Australia and Vermont.)

Margaret Morrow, *SUNY Plattsburgh*

Teaching Tips

Section 1.5

I prefer to teach this section immediately after introducing the Condorcet criterion. It reinforces head-to-head dynamics, and clearly illustrates how to create a method that satisfies Condorcet.

Counting is always challenging for students who have had no exposure to probability. I taught this course once with a "mini-excursion" into permutations and combinations before beginning the textbook. Without this type of platform, I emphasize that Copeland's method leads to impractical numbers of comparisons, without necessarily emphasizing how to count properly. There is no loss of continuity without the probability counting techniques for this chapter. Counting subsets is required for Chapter 2, which seems a more natural place to introduce the counting techniques.

Robert V. DeLiberato, *Saint Joseph's University*

■ ■ ■

Tell students it makes the work go faster if they figure out a majority so that they won't have to go through each column if someone gets the majority before then. Some students get confused because they think we're only looking at first-place votes, when actually it's the candidate ranked above another in each column, so even third place is better than fourth place, for example.

Margaret Michener, *University of Nebraska at Kearney*

■ ■ ■

Students confuse this method with determining whether there is a Condorcet candidate in an election. Emphasize that in determining the winner of an election by pairwise comparisons, one must compare each pair of candidates. By way of contrast, it is often not necessary to compare every pair of candidates when determining if there is a Condorcet candidate.

When teaching this method, emphasize that, when comparing two candidates, one counts how many times a candidate is listed higher than the other in each column of the preference schedule, even if the candidate does not receive the first place votes in that column.

Margaret Morrow, *SUNY Plattsburgh*

■ ■ ■

This method is time consuming. Do not do an example in class involving more than four players.

Tejinder S. Neelon, *California State University San Marcos*

■ ■ ■

1.5 The Method of Pairwise Comparisons

- So, What's Wrong with the Pairwise Comparisons?
- How Many Pairwise Comparisons?

1.6 Rankings

- Extended Ranking Methods
- Recursive Ranking Methods

Teaching Tips

Exercise 40 is also a great problem to assign. Students they need to really understand that there are a total of $\frac{N(N-1)}{2}$ comparisons when using pairwise comparison.

There are so many great real-world examples of voting. I always love teaching this material in a year when there is a presidential election. Several presidential elections over the last couple of decades have had a third-party candidate who has likely affected the outcome of the election, and this section is a great place to use political examples. There are also examples from the sporting world and the arts. Two great examples are the Academy Awards and the voting for the site of the Olympic Games. One of the groups of students who take this class at our school is theater majors. They always love the Academy Awards example. I explain the method used to choose the Best Picture by asking the class who were the five nominees in the most recent Academy Awards. Once we get the list, I make up a quota and some numbers to illustrate how the method works.

Deirdre Smith, *University of Arizona*

Section 1.6

I tend to view this section as supplemental material. Arrow's impossibility theorem can be introduced without this section, and I find it useful to proceed right to Arrow's theorem. I normally assign ranking methods as reading material, and ask students to be able to demonstrate knowledge of any one ranking method on a test. It seems to me that overemphasis of this particular section could detract from the chapter's conclusion.

Robert V. DeLiberato, *Saint Joseph's University*

■ ■ ■

I work on extended rankings the same class period that I go through pairwise comparisons. I then take one whole class period on recursive rankings, as these are pretty long and involved problems. I also like to find a problem where there is no Condorcet candidate to show how extended and recursive rankings can end up differently using pairwise comparisons.

Margaret Michener, *University of Nebraska at Kearney*

■ ■ ■

Instead doing this section separately, integrate this section with previous sections. Otherwise, you will end up doing many examples all over again.

Tejinder S. Neelon, *California State University San Marcos*

Teaching Tips

Section 2.1

It helps to introduce an example of a weighted voting system before proceeding to the abstract notation. In a democracy, students most naturally think "one person-one vote." I like to use the stock market as an example. Students can be directed to any of the financial websites to determine how many shares of stock are owned by board members or officers of a large corporation. I ask them to think in terms of "one share-one vote," and they quickly relate to the concentration of power in a large corporation.

I find it is worthwhile to have students spend some time experimenting with quotas. I assign problems with players and weights and ask them to select different quotas and experiment with how the dynamics of the voting system change.

The presence of a dictator renders every other player a dummy. When voting systems contain players with veto power, there may, or not be, dummies in the system. It is better to invest time at this stage assigning examples and requiring them to identify dummies. It helps the later stages of the chapter flow more smoothly.

Robert V. DeLiberato, *Saint Joseph's University*

■ ■ ■

I make up enough examples of weighted voting systems so that students understand what each number of the system represents, and why there must be restrictions on the amount of the quota or the system wouldn't work in real-life situations. It is important throughout the chapter that students understand that N is the number of players in the system. Students may snicker when I use the term "dummy," but maybe when they find out it means they don't have any power, they will study harder so they don't end up being dummies! I emphasize that there may be more than one person with that designation, and I also tell them that when we get to the Banzhaf method they will be able to tell that way who has veto power and who is a dummy instead of just be trying to figure it out in their heads.

Margaret Michener, *University of Nebraska at Kearney*

■ ■ ■

I start this material by asking the students to tell me all the situations that they can think of in which one person or group has more power than another. They almost always come up with examples like shareholders in companies, bosses, parents, teachers, and designated tie breakers (like the Vice President in the U.S. Senate). Occasionally they have come up with some funny ones. One student once said wives!

I give several examples which lead students to telling me what the basic assumptions would be.

Deirdre Smith, *University of Arizona*

Chapter 2
The Mathematics of Power

2.1 An Introduction to Weighted Voting

- Notation and Examples

2.2 The Banzhaf Power Index

- A Brief Mathematical Detour
- Shortcuts for Computing Banzhaf Power Distributions

2.3 Applications of the Banzhaf Power Index

Teaching Tips

Section 2.2

The first time I taught the course, I expected the calculation of the Banzhaf power index to be cumbersome, so I invested a lot of time in defining terms and detailing examples of the steps in the calculation. I learned that the fundaments of set theory, knowing the formula for the number of proper subsets, and showing a systematic way of listing all the proper subsets was the most critical part of the section. In the author's language, I recommend "taking the detour" before attempting the language of coalitions and the calculation of the power index.

Robert V. DeLiberato, *Saint Joseph's University*

■ ■ ■

I explain *critical players* by adding up the weights of the other players in the coalition, and if this is less than the quota, that person is a critical player. If that person isn't critical, then no one else in the coalition is either since it goes in descending order of the players' weights. Students definitely have trouble finding all the winning coalitions when there are five or more players. It helps for go through each possibility in a systematic order, starting with the fewest players. For example, to go through all the four-player coalitions, here's the order to try: $\{P_1, P_2, P_3, P_4\}$, $\{P_1, P_2, P_3, P_5\}$, $\{P_1, P_2, P_4, P_5\}$, $\{P_1, P_3, P_4, P_5\}$, $\{P_2, P_3, P_4, P_5\}$. I also explain that if they are having trouble finding who has veto power and who is a dummy, they can use Banzhaf. If players are critical in every winning coalition, they have veto power. If they are never a critical player, they are dummies.

Margaret Michener, *University of Nebraska at Kearney*

■ ■ ■

I use Pascal's triangle to show that the total number of coalitions for Banzhaf is $2^N - 1$.

Deirdre Smith, *University of Arizona*

Section 2.3

The text applications are good. Because I used corporate websites earlier to illustrate power, I like to assign students an open-ended assignment of creating their own corporations—one in which power is somewhat evenly distributed, and one in which power is concentrated in the hands of a few (while avoiding dictators). Making up their own systems seems to make this material more accessible to them.

Robert V. DeLiberato, *Saint Joseph's University*

■ ■ ■

This is a reading section for applying the Banzhaf method.

Margaret Michener, *University of Nebraska at Kearney*

Teaching Tips

Section 2.4

My suggestions for this section parallel those of Section 2.2. The detour is the lynchpin of the section. Make sure students understand the generalized counting principle (called the "multiplication rule" in the textbook) before proceeding. Once again, "take the detour" first. When I first started teaching, I had a natural resistance to interrupting the flow of the course to teach what appeared to be "prerequisite material." Now, when I encounter these types of detours, I make sure I have them examined thoroughly before I move forward with introducing the course's "main plot line."

Robert V. DeLiberato, Saint Joseph's University

■ ■ ■

To start on the Shapley-Shubik method, first go over what $N!$ means. Show how quickly this number grows and is therefore a disadvantage with four or more players. Again, go in pairs in a sequential order increasing numerically one time, then switching the last two players for the second in the pair. Double check that when the fractions are done, the sum of the numerators equals the denominator (same with the Banzhaf method).

Margaret Michener, University of Nebraska at Kearney

■ ■ ■

I use Pascal's triangle to show that the total number of coalitions for the Banzhaf method is $2^N - 1$ and trees to show that total number of sequential coalitions for the Shapley-Shubik method is $N!$.

Deirdre Smith, University of Arizona

Section 2.5

The Electoral College example is interesting, but the fact that students cannot apply concepts learned because of the sheer magnitude of the calculations makes it a bit less accessible. It's a nice way to wrap up the chapter. I like a variation of this scenario, where one makes the assumption that certain states are solid "red" or "blue" states, and focus on the power of the "swing" states in a general election. The role of Ohio and Florida as pivotal players quickly becomes evident and the calculations are feasible, under the assumptions created.

Robert V. DeLiberato, Saint Joseph's University

■ ■ ■

This is a reading section. Point out the applet in MyMathLab that students can go to for applications of the Shapley-Shubik power index.

Margaret Michener, University of Nebraska at Kearney

2.4 The Shapley-Shubik Power Index

- The Multiplication Rule and Factorials
- Back to the Shapley-Shubik Power Index

2.5 Applications of the Shapley-Shubik Power Index

Chapter 3
The Mathematics of Sharing

Teaching Tips

Section 3.1

Students are usually pretty interested in this chapter because everyone hates to feel they are being cheated, but to understand the chapter thoroughly, first they need to know the elements of fair-division problems and what each represents. I go through each of the three types of fair division, saying if the objects can't be cut without losing their value, the fair-division game is discrete.

Margaret Michener, *University of Nebraska at Kearney*

■ ■ ■

To increase interest and motivation for this topic, have students create problems using items they or their families own to supplement the exercise set or for an in-class activity.

This topic may be very relevant to student's lives, and some of them may want to share experiences in which distributions were made in their families in ways that were considered unfair. A discussion like this may motivate the need for a method of fair division of property, but be wary of getting into uncomfortable situations related to divorces in their families.

Abby Tanenbaum

Section 3.2

Since most people would prefer to be choosers in the divider-chooser method (if one side clearly is worth more, they will choose that side), to keep everything fair, make it random who is the divider and who is the chooser, for example, by flipping a coin.

Margaret Michener, *University of Nebraska at Kearney*

Section 3.3

There are lots of possibilities for the values the choosers bid on items, so I go through each example in the book from this section. Tell students the best way to do a distribution is to start by giving the chooser with the fewest choices his or her fair share first, then the next chooser with the least choices, and so on. The divider gets what's left over since he cut it equally, not knowing which he would end up with. However, make sure to go over how to use the divider-chooser method when two choosers both want the same piece and they don't list any other choices.

Margaret Michener, *University of Nebraska at Kearney*

Section 3.4

This is almost the opposite of lone divider. A quick review of angle measure from geometry will help students understand which pieces are fair shares.

Margaret Michener, *University of Nebraska at Kearney*

Teaching Tips

Section 3.5

So that students can keep track of which player gets a fair share in each round, I have them write out all the players and then cross them out one by one as they get their fair shares. Many students mistakenly believe that since P_1 cuts in the first round, then P_2 should cut in the second round, so go over this carefully with them that P_1 cuts in each round until he gets his fair share. Also, for the homework exercises on this section, make sure students know that they must diminish each slice to $\frac{1}{N}$ unless they are the last player.

Margaret Michener, *University of Nebraska at Kearney*

Section 3.6

I do a lot of examples from other book sources because, even though the method of sealed bids is not difficult, there are a lot of steps involved and most students have never used this method before and need lots of practice.

Margaret Michener, *University of Nebraska at Kearney*

Section 3.7

With Example 3.11, I go through the reasoning of what the players are thinking when they place their markers. Point out that this method works best when there are a lot more items than players and that most items should be approximately equal in value. If there is a tie, a coin toss will break the tie.

Margaret Michener, *University of Nebraska at Kearney*

Chapter 4
The Mathematics of Apportionment

4.1 Apportionment Problems

- Apportionment: Basic Concepts and Terminology

Teaching Tips

Section 4.1

I tell my students that this chapter will sound like a social studies chapter at times, given the men involved and the history of apportionment in the U.S. For both standard divisors and standard quotas, I tell students to round to hundredths place if necessary. Go over rounding, and make sure they don't double round (12.449 is closer to 12, not 12.5, and, therefore, 13). Sometimes they need to go further than hundredths in order to round correctly to the nearest integer. Practice making up problems for them to figure lower and upper quotas, because if they get these wrong, they will not do well in this chapter.

Margaret Michener, *University of Nebraska at Kearney*

■ ■ ■

Students seem to find the material of this chapter interesting. At the end of the chapter I do spend a little time discussing the Huntington Hill method (see Mini-Excursion 1), since this in the method currently used. Students seem able to grasp the rounding method for Huntington-Hill, and appreciate its significance for smaller states. (I do not ask students to actually determine an appropriate divisor using Huntington Hill.)

There are several useful sites with information on apportionments of seats for the House of Representatives: See http://www.nationalatlas.gov/articles/boundaries/a_conApport.html and www.wikipedia.org/wiki/United_States_congressional_apportionment).

In discussing apportionment problems different from the apportionment of seats in the House of Representatives, it is important to stress that these problems involve sharing out *indivisible* objects; some students miss this point. Students seem to enjoy discussing the significance of the number of seats allocated to each of the states. In particular, they are interested in the relation between the apportionment of seats in the House of Representatives and the number of Electoral College votes for each state.

Margaret Morrow, *SUNY Plattsburgh*

■ ■ ■

Use the Internet as a source of additional information about apportionment and the U.S. Census. Excellent information can be found on this page on the U.S. Census website: http://www.census.gov/population/www/censusdata/apportionment.html. Here you will find extensive information on the history of apportionment of the U.S. House of Representatives, a map showing the current apportionment and the changes that came about as a result of the most recent U.S. Census, and state-specific historical charts on population trends and how the number of representatives assigned to that state has changed over time. You might use this source to provide additional information and graphics for your presentations on this topic or for student research.

Abby Tanenbaum

Teaching Tips

Section 4.2

Remind students that once each state is given its lower quota, these numbers must be added up to see how many more seats are needed to get the final apportionment. Fairness criteria were discussed in a previous chapter, so when going over the quota rule, you can say it satisfies fairness criteria in a sense.

Margaret Michener, *University of Nebraska at Kearney*

■ ■ ■

Students can easily determine the winner of an election by this method using only a calculator. Here is an interesting historical fact: The first presidential veto in the United States was George Washington's veto of a bill proposing that Hamilton's method be used to apportion seats in the first House of Representatives. (Jefferson's method was adopted instead.)

Margaret Morrow, *SUNY Plattsburgh*

Section 4.3

Since no method is perfect, this section discusses disadvantages of Hamilton's method. In each paradox, point out what is being changed from the original table and which state loses because of it even though they should not lose a seat. I make up a new example not in the book, and have students guess which paradox it is and why.

Margaret Michener, *University of Nebraska at Kearney*

■ ■ ■

Students are suitably surprised by the paradoxes.

Margaret Morrow, *SUNY Plattsburgh*

Section 4.4

This section and the next are methods many students don't like because trial and error is used to come up with a suitable divisor. There is a formula you can use to approximate the divisor, but it usually goes okay just to try a number lower than the standard divisor. You can tell right away if you're way off and then adjust accordingly. Here is a formula if you'd like to use it for the Jefferson's modified divisor: Let I = integer part of largest state's standard quota. Then modified divisor = (largest state's population) $\div (I + 1)$, or try dividing by $(I + 2)$. This should work or at least be close.

Margaret Michener, *University of Nebraska at Kearney*

■ ■ ■

I have students use a spreadsheet to determine the appropriate modified divisor for Jefferson's method, as doing this using only a calculator is a little tedious. If spreadsheets are not available, you might want to provide a few potential divisors (for example, in Exercises 23–29), and ask the students to decide which divisor works, rather than expecting them to find an appropriate divisor from scratch. Incidentally, many students do not realize that more than one modified divisor can give an appropriate solution.

Margaret Morrow, *SUNY Plattsburgh*

■ ■ ■

4.2 Hamilton's Method and the Quota Rule

- The Quota Rule

4.3 The Alabama and Other Paradoxes

- The Population Paradox
- The New-States Paradox

4.4 Jefferson's Method

- Jefferson's Method and the Quota Rule

4.5 Adams's Method

4.6 Webster's Method

Teaching Tips

Most students have little trouble understanding and using the quota methods. They have more difficulty with the divisor methods. Many struggle with the modified divisor. I emphasize how they know when they should be rounding the modified divisor by making it a larger or smaller number, but tell them that the number they end up using will be found through a certain amount of trial and error. I make sure that they understand that there is not just one modified divisor that works; there is a range of numbers that work. Many of the students who take this class think there is always a magic formula in mathematics that will tell them the answer and are therefore somewhat frustrated by the fact that they have to make an educated guess about the modified divisor and then check to see if it works. On tests, I tell them that if they do not get the right divisor after two tries to just explain how if works and I will give them most of the credit.

Deirdre Smith, *University of Arizona*

Section 4.5

If you use the same example as you had for Jefferson's method, try the same difference in the divisor as worked before. For example, with 50,000 as the standard divisor, and 49,500 working for Jefferson's, then try 50,000 for Adams. Even if it doesn't work, it will be close.

Margaret Michener, *University of Nebraska at Kearney*

■ ■ ■

I suggest not belaboring Adam's and Webster's methods too much. I simply briefly discuss how they differ from Jefferson's method.

Margaret Morrow, *SUNY Plattsburgh*

Section 4.6

Make sure to point out that the standard divisor sometimes works, so try it first. If it doesn't work, the modified divisor can either be raised or lowered, depending on the problem. Table 4-18 in the Conclusion is a good summary of all four methods. There are a lot of written essays that could be assigned for a grade or extra credit if student wanted to do research on this topic.

Margaret Michener, *University of Nebraska at Kearney*

■ ■ ■

I think it is important to cover the Huntington-Hill method of apportionment because it is the method that is currently used to apportion seats in the U.S. House of Representatives. (See Mini-Excursion 1.) Students struggle with the geometric mean. I try to emphasize the difference between the arithmetic mean and the geometric mean. I emphasize that other than what is being used as the basis of comparison for rounding up or down, Huntington-Hill is just like Webster's method.

Deirdre Smith, *University of Arizona*

Chapter 5
The Mathematics of Getting Around

5.1   Euler Circuit Problems

Teaching Tips

Section 5.1

The transition to graph theory from voting (in the case of the structure used for my course) or voting and apportionment (the structure of the text) is not a smooth one. Most students have not seen graph theory before this course. This introductory section is fine, and I can't think of a way to improve upon it, but students still have difficulty making the transition. I like to start by drawing simple graphs on the board and asking them to name the elements: they say "point" and I say "vertex"; they say "line" and I say "edge." It's nothing profound; it's simply a way to get the idea of the vocabulary.

Robert V. DeLiberato, *Saint Joseph's University*

■ ■ ■

This is basically a reading section to familiarize students with graph theory and Euler circuit models. Some students think this is a fun chapter, especially those who are right-brained, visual learners.

Margaret Michener, *University of Nebraska at Kearney*

■ ■ ■

We begin the course with this chapter. I start the chapter on the first day of class after I have gone through the course policy and syllabus. There is usually about 20 to 25 minutes left of class time. I do not want to get too heavily into the material on this day, so I give an overhead view of a street plan and ask them to work on this in pairs for about 10 minutes:

1. A city street crew is sent to the section of town represented on the map to repair potholes. Since every street must be inspected for potholes, the crew would like to find a route that travels down each street exactly once. Is it possible to find such a route? If not, explain why you think it cannot be done.
2. Another crew is sent to this same section of the city to install new stop signs on every street corner. What route should the crew take so that each intersection is visited exactly once? Is there more than one route that would achieve this goal? Explain.
3. What is the difference between these two problems?

(Make sure you use a street plan for which the answer to one of questions 1 and 2 is *yes* and the other is *no*.) I then ask my students to tell me what they think. I find this is a good introductory example. Each student gets to know at least one of the other students in the class. They also get to voice their opinions on something that they feel they can do. This sets the tone that maybe this class will not be too intimidating after all. I then end the period by telling them that the first example (looking for potholes) is what we will be studying in this chapter (Euler circuits) and the second (checking stop signs) is an example of what we will be studying in Chapter 6 (Hamilton circuits).

5.2 What Is a Graph?

5.3 Graph Concepts and Terminology

Teaching Tips

The next day I introduce all the terminology from Chapter 5 and some from Chapter 6 using lots of graphs to illustrate loops, bridges, paths, circuits, etc. I also talk about the Königsberg bridge problem and then draw the graph several different ways to illustrate that so long as the edges and vertices are the same and the vertices all have the same degree, it does not make any difference what the graph looks like. This surprises the students because this is not the way that graphs worked in their algebra classes. After introducing all the terms, I ask them to think up real-world examples. When someone comes up with one I put it into one of four categories: Euler circuits/paths, Hamilton circuits/paths, trees, and digraphs. I then ask my students to think about what would be the vertices and what would be the edges in each of these groups. This generally takes an entire class period. It is only after this that I officially start Chapter 5.

Deirdre Smith, *University of Arizona*

Section 5.2

I find that some of the graphs pictured in the text get too complicated too quickly. I like to start with two vertices, then two vertices with a single edge, then a loop, then three vertices with no edges, one edge, and two edges. I try to sequentially illustrate how the graphs can become more complicated while I am reinforcing the vocabulary, and also beginning to illustrate the counting concepts that will be needed later, such as asking, "How many edges can I connect to this vertex if it has to touch another vertex?"

Robert V. DeLiberato, *Saint Joseph's University*

■ ■ ■

This section and the next need to be gone over carefully with all the definitions. To demonstrate how different pictures can represent the same graph, when I go through Example 5.9 on the board, I also show two additional pictures that are different from what is illustrated in the book. I show the students how they can check to make sure they represent the same graph by finding the degree of each vertex (in Section 5.3).

Margaret Michener, *University of Nebraska at Kearney*

Section 5.3

It is useful to introduce the concept of bridges as early as possible because they are critical to the algorithms. I start with two vertices and an edge, and show a simple bridge, erase the bridge, and then demonstrate that the graph has become disconnected. I spend a fair amount of time gradually increasing the complexity of the graph and the number of vertices, and asking students to find bridges and find ways of disconnecting the graphs.

The graph concepts and terminology are clear and well highlighted, but I prefer to follow different sequencing in introducing the ideas. The teaching technique has to be visual. Once I have taught the concept of bridges, I proceed to paths, then Euler paths, then circuits, and then Euler circuits.

Robert V. DeLiberato, *Saint Joseph's University*

■ ■ ■

Teaching Tips

Make sure students understand that Euler paths and circuits use *every edge* exactly once. I make up examples different from the book for ones that are not paths and circuits and then explain why they are not. Also point out that no edge can be used twice.

Margaret Michener, *University of Nebraska at Kearney*

■ ■ ■

Be slow and deliberate in finding the Euler paths and circuits. I find that if you rush through the material and show students the correct answer immediately, they do not develop the skills needed for solving the homework problems. During in-class examples, have students guide you through which edges should be chosen and step in only when necessary. Once you have taught this course once, you condition yourself to see the answer immediately and can quickly forget that students do not know how to approach these problems. Slow down and let the students figure it out with your guidance.

Explain the basics of a graph, and the parts and types of graphs. Then carefully discuss graphs for which it may not be obvious into what category they fall. For example, a single vertex is a graph, and is considered to be a connected graph.

Ryan Sieve, *University of Kansas*

Section 5.4

This section is prelude. I assign it as reading material.

Robert V. DeLiberato, *Saint Joseph's University*

■ ■ ■

From the examples in this section, students will be eager to find out when a graph has an Euler circuit or path, instead of just guessing.

Margaret Michener, *University of Nebraska at Kearney*

■ ■ ■

Make it abundantly clear that you may not cross a square on the grid problems diagonally. Explain that this would be analogous to driving through a city block or your neighbor's backyard.

Ryan Sieve, *University of Kansas*

Section 5.5

My preferred method and sequence for teaching this section involves providing the students with lots of graphs and asking them to use the following sequence:

1. Determine if the graph is connected. If it is not connected, draw some bridges to connect it.
2. Count the number of vertices.
3. Count the number of edges.
4. Identify the degree of each vertex.
5. Identify the number of odd vertices.
6. Verify Euler's sum of degrees theorem.
7. Use Euler's circuit and path theorems to determine whether the graph will have Euler paths and Euler circuits.
8. Verify that no graph has an odd number of odd vertices.

5.6 Fleury's Algorithm

- Algorithms
- Fleury's Algorithm

Teaching Tips

Since this course requires no formal proofs, the emphasis is on using intuition to verify that the results of Euler's theorems always hold true. In the process, students are learning the theorems and practicing the skills and working with bridges.

Robert V. DeLiberato, *Saint Joseph's University*

■ ■ ■

I tell students that all three theorems listed in this section should be memorized because they are the heart of the chapter. The only way the theorems can work right is if students can count degrees correctly, so it may help to make up a worksheet of different graphs and have them count all the degrees of each vertex. They won't need to keep track of even vertices, but of the number of odd ones. Also remind them that for Euler paths, they need to start at an odd vertex and end up at the other odd vertex, so they should keep track not only of how many odd-degree vertices there are, but also of where they are.

Margaret Michener, *University of Nebraska at Kearney*

■ ■ ■

I draw three graphs on the board. One has two odd vertices, one has several odd vertices, and the last has all even vertices. I have my students decide if an Euler path or circuit exists in each case. I then go back to the Konigsberg bridge graph and have them again decide if an Euler circuit or path exists. At this point they are ready to come up with Euler's theorems on their own.

Deirdre Smith, *University of Arizona*

Section 5.6

The textbook examples are good and the steps in Fleury's algorithm are clearly identified. The approach I favor is to get students working on the algorithm as quickly as possible. So, I might draw three versions of the same graph on the board, partition the class into three teams, ask each team to designate a person to draw and a spokesperson, and require each team to begin with a different starting point. The teams then "compete" by erasing edges and following Fleury's algorithm until an Euler circuit or path is found. When completed, teams compare results and exchange ideas on what worked well and what did not work well. Similar techniques are used for Eulerizing paths in Section 5.7.

Robert V. DeLiberato, *Saint Joseph's University*

■ ■ ■

Some students want to number edges at the vertex instead of the middle of an edge. Euler's sum of the degrees theorem is a good check to make sure they have numbered all the edges because you know ahead of time how many there are.

Margaret Michener, *University of Nebraska at Kearney*

Teaching Tips

Section 5.7

This is a great section for future engineers because it turns a graph that is not eulerized into one that is by adding the correct edges. Tell students there are several ways a graph can be eulerized, just like answers will vary on how they number the graphs.

Margaret Michener, *University of Nebraska at Kearney*

■ ■ ■

Give better visual examples of the differences between a eulerization, a semi-eulerization, and an optimal semi-eulerization.

Ryan Sieve, *University of Kansas*

■ ■ ■

I find that the students have a lot of difficulty with eulerization. I do a few on the board, all rectangles. One is 3 blocks by 3 blocks (only 4 edges need to be added), the next 4 blocks by 3 blocks, and the last 4 blocks by 4 blocks. I then give them a worksheet with two graphs and have them do the eulerization. This takes one class session. I live in a neighborhood in Tucson that is famous for its Christmas displays. There are several hayrides around the neighborhood at this time of year. So I drew a map of the neighborhood and have the students pretend they own one of the hayrides and have them eulerize the neighborhood. They find it challenging but fun to do.

Deirdre Smith, *University of Arizona*

■ ■ ■

Most students find the standard applications of Euler circuits and paths (routing garbage pick-up, mail deliveries, security guard patrols, parades, etc.) not too interesting or compelling. But here is a new application that I think is very modern and cool: Google Street View. In order to map an entire city at the street view level, Google carves out the metropolitan area into sections. For each section, a car with a special 360-degree camera mounted on the roof is assigned to travel along the streets of that section. The goal is to sweep through the section covering every block. When a block has to be covered more than once, the camera is turned off to eliminate the need to edit out duplications. Obviously you want to design the routes with the minimum number of duplications. This is clearly a "eulerization" problem.

Peter Tannenbaum, *California State University—Fresno*

Chapter 6
The Mathematics of Touring

6.1 Hamilton Paths and Hamilton Circuits

Teaching Tips

Section 6.1

Define a *Hamilton path* and draw one; then define a *Hamilton circuit* and draw one. Emphasize that Hamilton paths and circuits are focused on *vertices*, or making sure that each point is visited. The text lists graphs and has a chart that delineates Euler paths and circuits from Hamilton paths and circuits for each figure. I have found that it seems to lessen confusion to shine the light most clearly on the new concept and what it is, rather than contrasting it with what it is not.

After the Hamilton concepts are clear, it makes sense to briefly revisit Euler paths and circuits with their emphasis on *edges* and then draw the contrasts.

Robert V. DeLiberato, *Saint Joseph's University*

■ ■ ■

Students often get Euler circuits and Hamilton circuits confused. They may seem to understand as you do each section, but put the problems together on a test and watch the confusion ensue. You really need to emphasize that Euler is all about the *edges* (like a mail carrier going down the street), while Hamilton is all about the *vertices* (like a UPS delivery truck making specific deliveries). When the Rolling Stones' manager figures out a tour schedule, do they go on every possible flight in the United States to get to 20 cities or do they just get to the 20 cities? Which kind of circuit would we be interested in here?

Alicia Gordon, *Meredith College*

■ ■ ■

Students like this chapter even better than Chapter 5 because it's easier to use every vertex without having to use every edge. Example 6.1 is a great way to compare Euler circuits with Hamilton circuits, especially since I give a test over both chapters together. Let students find out that if a graph has a Hamilton circuit, it also has a Hamilton path just by dropping off returning to the starting vertex.

Margaret Michener, *University of Nebraska at Kearney*

■ ■ ■

Throughout this chapter, encourage the students to use colored pencils or color pens to draw over the graphs. I have found that student can easily lose track of which edges they have chosen after a few selections. Encourage students to find more than one answer to the problems where appropriate. This reinforces critical thinking skills and helps with the homework.

Ryan Sieve, *University of Kansas*

■ ■ ■

Teaching Tips

I draw several graphs that illustrate that the degree of the vertices is not relevant when finding a Hamilton circuit or path. I then define a complete graph and we look at a K_2 through K_5 and look at the number of edges. This helps students see why there are $\frac{N(N-1)}{2}$ edges in a complete graph with N vertices. We then discuss the number of Hamilton circuits. I find the circuits for K_2, K_3, and K_4 (with their help) and then ask them to come up with all the circuits in K_5. I give them about five minutes and start asking how many they found. Generally several people will have found all 24. I then tell them that a K_6 graph has 120 Hamilton circuits. A few of them will see the factorial pattern at this point.

Deirdre Smith, *University of Arizona*

Section 6.2

Returning to a common theme of my teaching tips, don't neglect the fundamentals. Review factorials, if necessary; work through the counting techniques; review sound ways to count in a systematic fashion; relate it to fundamental reviews conducted earlier in the semester. If the students can count correctly and in the proper sequence, they will not have much difficulty applying the algorithm.

Be certain that students know what a *complete graph* is, how many edges are in a complete graph, and how many Hamilton circuits exist for each complete graph. Also make sure that they can write the circuits for complete graphs with 3, 4, and 5 vertices, recognize mirror-image circuits, and understand the logic of how to reduce the number of distinct circuits.

This is the most important section in the chapter. Invest the appropriate amount of time in it.

Robert V. DeLiberato, *Saint Joseph's University*

■ ■ ■

Don't gloss over rewriting Hamilton circuits starting at vertex A as the *designated reference point*. I used to quickly mention this as I finished an early example and we would go on to the next problem. While that is enough for some students, many wondered what I was doing and why. If they weren't paying attention for those ten seconds, they lost a major point. Slow down and really explain why and how they should rewrite their solutions such as B, D, A, F, C, B as A, F, C, B, D, A, and that this answer is the same as A, D, B, C, F, A.

Alicia Gordon, *Meredith College*

■ ■ ■

Teaching Tips

A major mistake students just learning Hamilton circuits make is starting with a different starting vertex and then counting it as a new circuit. Always keep the same starting vertex when writing them out. After explaining what complete graphs are, go over the formula $(N - 1)!$ for the total number in the graph. Students will go faster naming all the Hamilton circuits when they realize that all the vertices are connected to all other vertices, so they don't even have to look at the graph to make sure there is an edge connecting the vertices.

Margaret Michener, *University of Nebraska at Kearney*

Section 6.3

This is another prelude section that may be assigned as reading.

Robert V. DeLiberato, *Saint Joseph's University*

■ ■ ■

I like to use examples involving places students might actually go, whether they are cities in our state or errands to run on a Saturday.

Alicia Gordon, *Meredith College*

■ ■ ■

This section illustrates why traveling salesman problems are important to learn, with all the applications available. Go over weighted graphs and what optimal Hamilton circuits are. Smaller is better here, because we want the fastest time, shortest distance, or cheapest cost depending upon what the weights of the graph represent.

Margaret Michener, *University of Nebraska at Kearney*

Section 6.4

Emphasize that proper counting techniques should always be employed first to identify the scope of the problem and to appreciate whether a "brute-force" search for the optimal circuit is feasible.

Robert V. DeLiberato, *Saint Joseph's University*

■ ■ ■

I start on brute force with Example 6.7, explaining how I can go in alphabetical order to organize all 24 circuits in a complete graph with 5 vertices. Point out that there will always be a tie for the optimal Hamilton circuit, since the weight of the mirror-image circuit is the same that of the original circuit.

Margaret Michener, *University of Nebraska at Kearney*

Section 6.5

After discussing the nearest-neighbor algorithm, I go over advantages and disadvantages of both methods introduced in this section. This leads to the discussion of efficient algorithms and figuring the relative error. Make sure students don't write the mirror-image circuit as an answer when using the nearest-neighbor method.

Margaret Michener, *University of Nebraska at Kearney*

■ ■ ■

Teaching Tips

Throughout Sections 6.5–6.8, explain the different algorithms using examples. Then reiterate with student-led practice problems or group work. Challenge the students to find optimal solutions, Assign problems such that the students work each of the different types of algorithms (including nearest-neighbor *and* repetitive nearest neighbor). This helps illustrate why the "brute-force" algorithm earns its name and how the answer they obtain may not always be optimal.

Ryan Sieve, *University of Kansas*

■ ■ ■

When I start talking about the algorithms, of course I start with brute force. Students easily see how tedious and time-consuming this would be if there were several vertices. I then ask them how they choose their route when they have several errands to run. Someone always immediately comes up with the nearest-neighbor algorithm. My example illustrates how this can be rather shortsighted, and I ask what they could do to improve it.

Deirdre Smith, *University of Arizona*

Section 6.6

I found this to be a useful time to link the concepts in this chapter to some of the ideas in voting theory from Chapter 1. The Arrow impossibility theorem demonstrated that certain things are impossible. This chapter illustrates that brute force is capable of yielding an optimal solution, but computing capacity and time make the search for an efficient "less than optimal" solution a more expedient approach to the problem.

Encourage students to think about devising their own trial-and-error algorithms before introducing the algorithms in the text. The objective is to get them to recognize that brute force is not practical, and to engage them in suggesting alternatives, before they look ahead, if possible.

Robert V. DeLiberato, *Saint Joseph's University*

■ ■ ■

Computers can come in handy when doing brute force, but if you need to do it by hand, other methods may make more sense if a graph has 6 or more vertices.

Margaret Michener, *University of Nebraska at Kearney*

Section 6.7

Because the nearest-neighbor algorithm is an easy concept for students, repetitive nearest-neighbor doesn't usually give them many problems. However, sometimes they forget to rewrite the circuit with the lowest total weight to the same circuit with the specific required starting vertex. Go over this carefully.

Margaret Michener, *University of Nebraska at Kearney*

6.6 Approximate Algorithms

6.7 The Repetitive Nearest-Neighbor Algorithm

6.8 The Cheapest-Link Algorithm

Teaching Tips

Section 7.1

When covering networks, I find it useful to draw a point to represent each vertex. Having an actual point allows the students to identify the number of edges connected to a vertex more easily. I usually ask students to "count the spokes" when finding the degree of each vertex. In addition, I use an animated slide presentation that shows the sequence of edges being traversed. Another technique would be to use two different colors on the board: one for the original network and a second color with which to traverse it. Use arrows with the second color to show the direction in which it is traversed.

Kevin Chouinard, *Northern Virginia Community College*

■ ■ ■

By the time I reach this chapter, sufficient foundation exists for students to master this material rather easily. Trees are simpler than circuits, and this transition is a good example of the benefits of investing extra time in fundamentals earlier in the semester. I always find that I am able to move at a rapid pace in Chapter 7. I am also able to reassure students that the reasons for investing time in the "fruitless search for non-optimal algorithms" are about to become clear. Students usually find this chapter rewarding and are eager to work on problems that have an optimal solutions. It provides them with a sense of closure that they are more accustomed to having for math courses—there is a clear, unambiguous solution, at last.

Robert V. DeLiberato, *Saint Joseph's University*

■ ■ ■

Spend a lot of time on the properties that define *trees*. These can be used as criteria for determining if a graph is a tree or can have a tree.

Explain that is a graph is disconnected, you may not add an edge to connect and call it a tree. Trees can only be formed using existing edges.

Ryan Sieve, *University of Kansas*

■ ■ ■

I use the example of installing an irrigation system in my front yard as an example. Students quickly see why we do not what any circuits. I also have them draw their family tree and ask them what it would mean if there was a circuit in their family tree.

Deirdre Smith, *University of Arizona*

Section 7.2

Among my favorite problems in this section are the problems like Exercises 13–18. I talk about how they can figure out the number of trees without drawing them. This is quite difficult for the students, but with a few examples and lots of practice they get quite good at it. I always enjoy seeing their sense of pride when they actually get how to do this.

Deirdre Smith, *University of Arizona*

Chapter 7
The Mathematics of Networks

7.1 Trees
- Properties of Trees

7.2 Spanning Trees

Teaching Tips

Sections 7.3–7.5

My quick preview to Section 7.3 is that Kruskal's algorithm is "the cheapest-link algorithm with a happy ending." The methodology is easily connected to Section 6.8. Students learn the algorithm with little difficulty, and it is rewarding for them to see that this is an optimal algorithm.

Robert V. DeLiberato, *Saint Joseph's University*

■ ■ ■

Students seem to make fewer mistakes if, when finding a minimum spanning tree using Kruskal's method, they actually list the edges, smallest weight to largest, and systematically choose or not choose them in order. They seem to have a better understanding of the process and are less likely to fade into some sort of nearest-neighbor method where they feel they need to start at "vertex *A*" and/or feel the chosen edges must be connected.

Drill the rules for not choosing an edge into your students. While avoiding three edges from a single vertex seems to go well, they often don't notice when choosing an edge will create a circuit. Remind them that they are trying to find a *tree*, and thus they cannot have any "loops" at all. The instructions usually ask them to find a "minimum spanning *tree*," so they should know what they are looking for. They also seem to have a problem with knowing when to stop!

Alicia Gordon, *Meredith College*

■ ■ ■

Advise students to take their time when working on these sections. Most errors I encounter come from students that are in a rush and do not take time to look at the graph for the best possible solution.

Ryan Sieve, *University of Kansas*

Teaching Tips

Section 8.1

I have created "scheduling scrap paper" that I use throughout the scheduling chapter. It is basically paper with blank versions of the two-processor and three-processor schedules they see in the textbook. Many students benefit by being able to count out the boxes as they schedule the tasks. And it saves time in class because I don't have to wait for students to draw all the little boxes!

Julie March, *Onondaga Community College, SUNY*

■ ■ ■

Be deliberate and slow. This is very simple material, but nearly all mistakes occur when students do not go through the process to appropriately select and assign tasks.

For their work throughout this chapter, make sure students create a "method" or "checklist" for each task assignment iteration. This provides the students with a common reference and visual reminder to go through each step to identify the correct assignment.

Ryan Sieve, *University of Kansas*

■ ■ ■

I only cover the material in the beginning of the chapter. I find the algorithms to be somewhat complicated and I think that the students can get a good idea that the least amount of time it takes to complete a task is dictated by the longest path of the digraph by just setting up some digraphs. The example I use is "turning around an airplane." I ask them to tell me what needs to be done to turn around a plane, and after we come up with that list I ask them to estimate how long it takes to do each of these tasks. I then do an unrelated example where I put a given precedence table on the board and then we go through the digraph for this example. From this example we look at the idea of a critical path. I then go back to the airplane example. We set up the precedence table and digraph and then find the critical path.

Deirdre Smith, *University of Arizona*

Section 8.2

My students often confuse the terms "incident to" and "incident from" when I introduce directed graphs. I always suggest they replace "*A* is incident to *B*" with "*A* goes to *B*," and "*B* is incident from *A*" with "*B* comes from *A*." These substitutions help the students by providing a visualization of the direction of the arc.

Julie March, *Onondaga Community College, SUNY*

Section 8.3

When first scheduling with priority lists, some students will ignore the digraph and just schedule based on the order in the priority list. To avoid this, I often refer to the priority list as a "wish list." I tell them we would like to follow the priority list, but we can only do that if the digraph says it is okay. I also tell them that the digraph "trumps" the priority list.

Julie March, *Onondaga Community College, SUNY*

■ ■ ■

Chapter 8
The Mathematics of Scheduling

8.1 The Basic Elements of Scheduling

8.2 Directed Graphs (Digraphs)

8.3 Scheduling with Priority Lists

- The Priority-List Model

Teaching Tips

Ensure that students are comfortable with priority lists and precedence relations. Start small! Do examples that address specific rules one at a time. Students get lost in the priority lists and precedence relations if they are constantly assigning idle time and getting hung up on the rules. Work problems that are simple at first and gradually work into problems that contain more rules and relations.

Ryan Sieve, *University of Kansas*

Section 8.4

Due to the fact that the decreasing-time algorithm is so weak, my students will often "stray" from the priority list because they can see how to create a more efficient schedule. I have to remind them that they need to follow the priority list even if is not logical or efficient.

Julie March, *Onondaga Community College, SUNY*

Section 8.5

I think it is important to emphasize the connection between the critical time and the completion time of a project. Many students will initially state that since the critical path is the longest path in the project, then the critical time must be the longest completion time. After discussing critical times and critical paths, I have the students schedule a project that leads them to discover that the critical time is actually the shortest possible completion time.

Julie March, *Onondaga Community College, SUNY*

■ ■ ■

In this section and the next one, do *not* introduce the backflow algorithm and critical-path algorithm until students have had a chance to practice scheduling.

Ryan Sieve, *University of Kansas*

Section 8.6

Before "officially" teaching the critical-path algorithm, I give students a project to schedule in which they need to create the priority list they feel will provide the most efficient schedule. Now that they are familiar with critical times, many will instinctively use the critical-path algorithm.

Julie March, *Onondaga Community College, SUNY*

Section 8.7

I have my students schedule the same project with independent tasks over and over; adding an additional processor each time. Eventually they discover that the absolute minimal completion time for a schedule with independent tasks, no matter how many processors, is equal to the longest task.

Julie March, *Onondaga Community College, SUNY*

Section 9.1

I love teaching this chapter because of the surprising connections that emerge. It is also a rich topic for students to research. Many excellent online resources are available for this chapter.

Margaret Morrow, *SUNY Plattsburgh*

Section 9.2

This is a wonderful topic to help students notice and generalize patterns. Students find the F_N notation hard to understand. I find that it works very well to introduce this notation as follows: I give the students a grid of rectangles, and tell them to think of these as the pages of a book, and number them 1, 2, 3, etc. I then get the students to write the first Fibonacci number (1) on the first page, the second (1) on the second page, the third (2) on the third page, etc. I then introduce the notation using this; for example, F_3 is the Fibonacci number on the third page, so $F_3 = 2$. This seems to work well! (Note: This idea comes from the Vermont Mathematics Initiative (VMI)).

I always bring a bag of pine cones to class and have students count the spirals going in both directions when the cone is viewed from the top. The numbers of spirals are always Fibonacci numbers.

My students find it too daunting to calculate Fibonacci numbers via Binet's formula using a calculator. Instead I provide them with an *Excel* spreadsheet that does the calculation automatically. Students are somewhat surprised that the formula even yields an integer.

Margaret Morrow, *SUNY Plattsburgh*

■ ■ ■

When students begin using the F_N notation, have them write out the sequence of Fibonacci numbers with the corresponding F_N notation above it. This helps provide a visual reference to understand which Fibonacci number corresponds to which value of N. This has done wonders in explaining homework problems.

Draw more attention to the "friendlier" looking version of Binet's formula: $F_N = (A_N - B_N)/\sqrt{5}$.

Ryan Sieve, University of Kansas

■ ■ ■

Because of the applications to such diverse fields as art, architecture, music, and nature, this is an ideal lesson for projects. Have students or groups of students research applications of their choice and present their results to the class using visuals or music. Some students could also research the life of Fibonnaci and his contributions to mathematics.

Abby Tanenbaum

Chapter 9
The Mathematics of Spiral Growth

9.1   Fibonacci's Rabbits

9.2   Fibonacci Numbers

9.3 The Golden Ratio

- The Golden Property

Teaching Tips

Section 9.3

I warn the students to be critical of material related to the golden ratio that they find on the Internet, as claims of connections to the golden ratio are sometimes inflated and unsubstantiated.

I like to introduce the golden rectangle at the beginning of this section, to provide some relief from the algebra. I have a sheet showing six rectangles with different side ratios, only one of which is a golden rectangle. I give this to the students the class period before I introduce the golden rectangle. I ask them to ask five friends or relatives which of the rectangles they find most pleasing. At the next class I gather the statistics from the class; the golden rectangle has been the most popular choice every time I have tried this. I then tell them that rectangles of this particular shape are called *golden rectangles*, and that the ratio of longer to shorter side for this kind of rectangle is called the *golden ratio*, and this is approximately equal to 1.618. (One could instead have the students measure and estimate the ratio from the golden rectangle on their sheet.) The golden ratio is denoted by the Greek letter ϕ (phi), after the fifth century Greek sculptor Phidias.

I think it is worth spending some time on using the quadratic formula to solve quadratic equations, and on using a calculator to obtain a decimal approximation for the answers. This strengthens the student's algebra skills. Many of the students in my class find this hard, and need quite a lot of help and practice with it.

I like to motivate how the equation $x^2 = x + 1$ relates to the golden ratio at this point (though one must take care not to frighten the students with the algebra here). They seem able to follow if when it is presented as follows:

Suppose a line segment is divided into two parts, a longer part (length ℓ) and a shorter part (length s).

The key feature of the golden ratio is that the ratio of the longer to the shorter part is equal to the ratio of the whole to the longer: $\frac{\ell}{s} = \frac{\ell + s}{\ell}$ (Equation (1)).

For simplicity in calculating the ratio, let's take the length of the shorter piece as length 1, which means that for a segment divided in the golden ratio, the longer piece will have length exactly ϕ (since the ratio will now be $\frac{\phi}{1}$). Students seem able to accept the validity of this simplification when I ask them to imagine just reducing the segment on a photocopy machine until the shorter segment has length 1.

Equation (1) then becomes $\frac{\phi}{1} = \frac{\phi + 1}{\phi}$, and multiplying both sides by ϕ gives $\phi^2 = \phi + 1$.

Margaret Morrow, *SUNY Plattsburgh*

Teaching Tips

Section 9.4

I regard the section on gnomons as a good opportunity to have the students think about similar figures, and practice setting up and solving simple algebraic equations (such as in Exercise 43).

Most of my students do not know that if the linear dimensions of a figure are multiplied by a scale factor c, then the area of the figure will be multiplied by a factor of c^2. (See Exercises 35–38.) I provide them with similar polygons of different shapes drawn on quad paper to explore this idea. (One square region on the quad paper is taken as one of unit of area.)

Margaret Morrow, *SUNY Plattsburgh*

■ ■ ■

Exercise 37 seems to give students problems because of the conflicting units. This is a great opportunity to show how the units cancel out and the importance of setting up the ratio correctly.

Explain very clearly that a ring can *not* have a gnomon. Rings may only be gnomons to other shapes.

When working on problems like Example 9.7, students are easily confused in setting up their ratios. If they are given a consistent format there seems to be fewer problems. This is particularly useful for the triangle problems.

Ryan Sieve, *University of Kansas*

Section 9.5

The growth of a human being provides a good example of nongnomonic growth. On the other hand, the leaves of plants usually display gnomonic growth.

Margaret Morrow, *SUNY Plattsburgh*

9.4 Gnomons

- Golden and Fibonacci Rectangles

9.5 Spiral Growth in Nature

- Gnomonic Growth

Chapter 10
The Mathematics of Money

10.1 Percentages

10.2 Simple Interest
- Simple Interest

10.3 Compound Interest
- The General Compounding Formula
- The Annual Percentage Yield (APY)

Teaching Tips

Section 10.1

Students never seem to have any intuitive difficulty expressing fractions as percentages. In dealing with financial expressions, the most common difficulty I have encountered is consistently converting smaller percentages to a proper decimal for calculations. It is worth investing some time on how a mortgage rate of "7 and $\frac{3}{4}$ percent" would properly be expressed in decimal form as 0.0775. The hybrid fraction included in the percentage calculations seems to cause confusion.

Markups and markdowns seem to be handled most easily when they are described as synonymous with percentage increases and percentage decreases. My sequence for teaching this is:

1. Express percentages as decimals.
2. Increases are positives; decreases are negatives.
3. Add to the decimal to obtain the appropriate multiplicative factor.
4. The terms then can be multiplied together in any desired order.
5. This also solves the decrease dilemma. Students can see that and this is clearly the maximum possible decrease.

Robert V. DeLiberato, *Saint Joseph's University*

Sections 10.2 and 10.3

I pass around a sheet of paper at the start of class. Starting with $1000, each student calculates 10% interest and adds it to the amount, then passes on the paper. At the end, we compare the compound interest for years to simple interest over the same time period. I also bring in ads that show the APY, so students see that it is really used.

MaryAnne Anthony, *Santa Ana College*

■ ■ ■

I have students identify all variables before substituting them into the general compounding formula, $F, P, r, n,$ and t. After students substitute values in the formula, I show them how to enter the expression into the calculator, making sure order of operations is correctly performed. This helps to avoid rounding errors, which is very important when completing homework in MyMathLab.

Molly L. Beauchman, *Yavapai College*

■ ■ ■

When entering interest formulas into the calculator, I verbalize and perform each step. Students who are unfamiliar with the keystrokes will become frustrated easily if the instructor inputs the information at too fast a pace.

Norma Biscula, *University of Maine, Augusta*

■ ■ ■

Teaching Tips

Average daily balance is the most difficult concept in Section 10.2. Some students may not be familiar with the type of weighted average used in its calculation, having only worked with basic averages in the past. Stress why the weighted average is necessary.

In comparing simple and compound interest, emphasize that with compound interest, interest in calculated on the principal *plus any previously earned interest.* For a first example of compound interest, I like to choose one in which the interest is only compounded twice, and, for the sake of comparison, I like to use the same numbers as in a problem done earlier with simple interest. Having a direct comparison allows the students to concretize the differences between simple and compound interest.

Kevin Chouinard, *Northern Virginia Community College*

■ ■ ■

Simple interest is linear, while compound interest is exponential. Do a quick review of linear and exponential functions and demonstrate the differences. I rely more on students' prior knowledge of the forms and properties of the underlying mathematical functions than on memorizing formulas.

Use a simple example for general compounding: Show how $100 accumulates at the end of one year if the 6% nominal rate is compounded annually, semiannually, quarterly, monthly, daily, and continuously. Let the concept of continuous compounding be intuitively grasped as the limiting case of discrete compounding, and then show the two relevant formulas.

Robert V. DeLiberato, *Saint Joseph's University*

■ ■ ■

For the most part, students are able to set up the problems correctly; they are just unsure on how to put the formula in their calculators. For the first few problems, I walk them through it step-by-step. Because there are typically two or three different calculators being used in the class, I show students how to input the problem step-by-step. For the general compounding formula, I start with the fraction first, then add, raise it to the power, and then multiply by the principal.

LaRonda Oxendine, *Robeson Community College*

■ ■ ■

Explain compounding with the "General Compounding Formula" on page 374. Students seemed to get confused between the annual and general compounding formulas. when they are essentially the same thing. The general formula provides all the components and forces the student to recognize the effects of compounding.

Ryan Sieve, *University of Kansas*

■ ■ ■

I teach this chapter so that it culminates in the major project in the course, a mock buying of a house. The project incorporates compound interest, annuities and amortization, all of which are covered in the text. It also includes having the student set up a budget and research closing costs on buying a house. Students are asked to find property taxes and insurance, etc for the home they buy. A useful website is www.realestate.com.

When I do examples in this section for simple and compound interest, I use real world data. My favorite example is to use the national debt to compute interest.

Deirdre Smith, *University of Arizona*

■ ■ ■

10.4 Geometric Sequences

- The Geometric Sum Formula

10.5 Deferred Annuities: Planning Savings for the Future

Teaching Tips

Some students may need a considerable amount of help in learning to use their calculators efficiently to do the calculations required in this chapter, especially when complicated exponential expressions are involved. Plan to spend time on this in class.

Abby Tanenbaum

Section 10.4

Showing the derivation of the geometric sequence formula seems to help students relate to it and remember it more easily. This is one of the few instances where showing students the proof in an introductory course of this nature helps facilitate the application of the underlying theory.

Robert V. DeLiberato, *Saint Joseph's University*

■ ■ ■

Ensure you point out at that in the geometric sum formula, the last term has exponent $N - 1$, while the exponent in the expression for the sum is N. Students always make a mistake between the N and $N - 1$ as the exponent.

Ryan Sieve, *University of Kansas*

Section 10.5

Drawing timelines is the easiest way to illustrate annuity concepts. Draw a horizontal line with tick marks and label each tick mark with a number from 0 to N. Highlight 0 as present value and N as future value. Place the amount of the annuity payment at each tick mark, and then show how geometric series formulas can be used to express the present and future values.

Robert V. DeLiberato, *Saint Joseph's University*

■ ■ ■

I also do an example in the annuity section on saving for retirement. Students are quite impressed in this section by how much of the final amount is interest and how much their contribution. I also do the same example where they start saving at age 25 as opposed to starting to save the same amount at age 50. This helps them see how important it is to start saving for retirement as early as possible.

I find the biggest problem students have in this section is entering the formulas correctly on their calculators. I make sure that all students bring their calculators with them to class every day while covering this material. I go through entering the formulas step-by-step in class. I also make sure I am available after class for those students who are still having difficulty. They generally have an easier time entering the formulas if they use a graphing calculator.

Deirdre Smith, *University of Arizona*

Teaching Tips

Section 10.6

For this section, I ask students to bring in an advertisement for a dream car they would like to purchase. I have a sample from the newspaper that includes interest rates for different financing options from a local bank. We work through buying a car together—how the bank looks at the loan as a compound interest problem and how the customer looks at the loan as an annuity with a monthly payment. We use the formula and then I show students how to use the TI-84 Plus for an amortized loan. Students then work in pairs to determine the monthly payment for their cars, using either the finance information from their advertisement or the finance information I have available. We also talk about how to determine the price of a car they can afford if they estimate their monthly payments.

We construct an amortization schedule for the car using spreadsheet software as a demonstration. I then have students construct the first few lines of the amortization schedule "by hand" for their cars.

I also ask the question, "If you want to pay off your car loan after two years, what is the unpaid balance of the loan?" We calculate this together using the formula for the class example and students calculate using their cars. I show them how to use a website mortgage calculator (www.bankrate.com) to find the payments, amortization schedule, and unpaid balance. (The graphing calculator will construct an amortization table, but it is a more cumbersome process.)

Molly L. Beauchman, *Yavapai College*

■ ■ ■

Students are surprised at how much interest is paid in an installment loan. We discuss advertisements from companies that say, "Pay no interest for months" and what that means if the balance is not paid in the time given.

Most students have a credit card. I have students bring in a copy of one of their monthly statements, determine the method used for determining finance charges, calculate their finance charge for the month, and compare to their actual finance charge on the statement.

Norma Biscula, *University of Maine, Augusta*

■ ■ ■

When working with the formula for the monthly payment on a mortgage, I usually do the same example twice. One calculation is for the students with scientific calculators and the other is for those with graphing calculators. Since the formula is intricate, the calculations are very different and students sometimes have difficulty adapting the methods from one machine to the other.

Calculating the total interest paid on a mortgage often causes great surprise for the students when they see that the total interest paid is usually greater than the amount borrowed!

Kevin Chouinard, *Northern Virginia Community College*

■ ■ ■

Teaching Tips

The amount of an installment loan is always the present value of a geometric series. Use the timeline concept and demonstrate that an installment loan is simply a specific type of an annuity problem. I don't find the introduction of new notation and formulas to be helpful to mastering this concept.

Robert V. DeLiberato, *Saint Joseph's University*

■ ■ ■

I also like to do examples where students tell me how much they think they will spend on a car and a house when they are ready to buy these. I then use these numbers to compute the monthly payments if they were to buy a car and house worth these amounts. They usually tell me they are planning on buying a $25,000–$30,000 car and a house for about $300,000. They are always pretty surprised to find out what this will cost in monthly payments! I also talk about how much of this is interest and how much goes towards paying for the house. This also quite freaks them out. I have had many students come to the conclusion that buying a house is a rip-off, so I then discuss the advantages of home ownership.

When you think about it, most people are making some type of payment (whether it is a house, car, or furniture payment). I start out with the following example: I buy a new car and I finance $28,000 at 7% for 6 years. My monthly car payment is $477.37. How much will I have paid for this car at the end of 6 years? As we begin to work through this problem, students begin to ask about paying more than the required payments and paying the car off early. Once this occurs, we can begin to talk about principal and interest. After our discussion, I ask them to think about the payments they are currently making. I ask them to spend some time figuring out how they will end up paying for the item(s).

I start the discussion of home mortgages about the same way I do the discussion of car loans. I ask the following question: I have purchased a new house with a $160,000 mortgage at a fixed rate of 6.25% for 30 years. My monthly house payment for principal and interest is $985.15. In addition to my down payment, how much do you think I will have paid for this house at the end of 30 years? I always get a range of answers. Some say $200,000, while others think it may be as high as $300,000. Then we work through the problem. Many of the students are surprised by the final answer. I also show them how much of their first payment is applied to the principal and how much of it is interest. Once again they start asking about paying more than the required monthly payment each month. I have an Internet connection in my classroom, so I find a mortgage calculator and we play around with some numbers. They are amazed at the fact that just paying $100 more each month can cut the length of their loan by around $6\frac{1}{2}$ years.

LaRonda Oxendine, *Robeson Community College*

■ ■ ■

When I am in a classroom with an Internet connection, I connect to a mortgage calculator. This way they can see how paying more each month can dramatically reduce the number of years they need to pay off the loan.

Deirdre Smith, *University of Arizona*

Teaching Tips

Section 11.1

I introduce this chapter by displaying overhead transparencies showing patterns or architectural features with symmetries. (Patterns by M.C. Escher are particularly good for this.) The students willingly agree that the patterns "have symmetry." I then ask them what they mean by saying the pattern is symmetric, or I ask, "If someone in the class did not agree that the figure was symmetric, how would you convince them?" Students invariably come up with the idea that in the case of a figure with reflection symmetry, one could fold the pattern along the mirror line to show that the two sides match. They find it a little harder to suggest rotating the pattern to make it fit on top of itself in the case where the pattern has rotational symmetry only, but someone has always eventually suggested that. I point out that this implies that in order to understand and classify symmetries, we need first to study rigid motions in the plane. This serves to motivate studying the rigid motions in the plane.

Margaret Morrow, *SUNY Plattsburgh*

Section 11.2–11.4

In order to do the rotations, provide tracing paper (or parchment paper) so students can physically see the rotations.

Linda Padilla, *Joliet Junior College*

■ ■ ■

Encourage students to obtain graph paper to draw the figures in the book. Many errors come from attempting to work poor representations of the figures. This tends to confuse and frustrate the students.

Encourage students to use colored pencils or multiple colors of pen to help draw flipped, rotated, translated, or any intermediate figures.

Use shapes and assign numbers or letters to the vertices to illustrate proper and improper motion.

The motions outlined in this chapter provide many opportunities for humor, whether you as the instructor mimic the motions, or call upon students to act them out.

Ryan Sieve, *University of Kansas*

■ ■ ■

Students will be much more successful with the material in these sections if they perform the various transformations physically than if they just look at the figures in the textbook. Either provide models for students to use of have them draw and cut out cardboard figures in class to use for this purpose.

Abby Tanenbaum

Chapter 11
The Mathematics of Symmetry

11.5 Glide Reflections

11.6 Symmetry as a Rigid Motion

Teaching Tips

Section 11.5

Students tend to forget that for a glide reflection, the translation vector must be parallel to the axis of reflection. Also it is useful for the later work on symmetry to stress that the same result is obtained when one first translates, then reflects, as when one first reflects, then translates. (See Figure 11-15.) The latter seems to be the most helpful way to think about glide reflections later in the chapter when trying to identify glide-reflection symmetry.

Students are naturally puzzled about why we include glide reflections as a separate rigid motion, while we do not include, for example, "rotation reflections." The reason is that provided we do include glide reflections., then given any starting and ending position for a figure in the plane, we can describe the motion from starting to ending position by just one rigid motion (that is, one of reflection, rotation, translation, or glide reflection). If we leave out glide reflections, we can no longer do this.

Margaret Morrow, *SUNY Plattsburgh*

■ ■ ■

Make it very clear a glide translation *must* have the axis parallel to the vector. This will be particularly important when explaining patterns in Section 11.7.

Ryan Sieve, *University of Kansas*

Section 11.6

For rotational symmetry, I find it helpful to have the students consider not only the angle of rotational symmetry, but also the *order* of rotational symmetry (the number of distinct ways that the pattern falls on top of itself when rotated). For some examples, students find it easier to use the order of rotational symmetry to determine the angle of rotational symmetry than to determine the angle of rotational symmetry directly. The order of rotational symmetry is also helpful when classifying patterns using the Z notation.

I have small mirrors, MIRAs (the MIRA™ geometry tool), transparency sheets, and overhead transparency markers available so that students can check whether certain symmetries are present. Many students really need these aids to train their eyes to spot the symmetries.

When classifying patterns using Z or D notation, one needs to stress that if the pattern has reflection symmetry, then it is classified as a D type, and not a Z type, even though it has rotational symmetry as well. (Students tend to provide both a D classification and Z classification in this case.) In this system, the D stands for *dihedral*, which is appropriately suggestive of reflection symmetry.

I have several sheets showing complex, finite figures (often called rosette patterns) from different cultures. I ask the students to identify for each figure all lines of symmetry and all angles of rotational symmetry. Finally I ask the students to determine the symmetry type of each figure. Students seem to respond well to this activity. (An Internet search for "Celtic patterns" or "Native American patterns" provides a good start on a collection of patterns.)

Margaret Morrow, *SUNY Plattsburgh*

■ ■ ■

11.7 Patterns

- Wallpaper Patterns

Teaching Tips

The symmetry notation D_N, Z_N, D_∞ has always confused students for some reason. Instruct students to draw the figures in their homework and illustrate the symmetries, labeling reflections or rotations.

Ryan Sieve, *University of Kansas*

Section 11.7

As in Section 11.6, I find that many students need aids such as MIRAs and overhead transparencies to check for the presence of symmetries.

When asking students to analyze border patterns printed on a page, I find that I need to stress that one must imagine the pattern repeating itself in both directions off the printed figure. It takes some students a little while to understand that it might be tricky to spot the position of lines of symmetry, or centers of rotational symmetry in a border or wallpaper pattern. (For example, an axis of vertical reflection symmetry might not be centered in the section of the border pattern printed on a page.) Of all the possible symmetries for border patterns, it is glide reflection symmetry that students find hardest to identify. Also, when classifying border patterns, many students have difficulty distinguishing between types 1g and 12; it is helpful to have students check for the presence of rotational or glide reflection symmetry using a tracing of the pattern on an overhead transparency.

The following decision procedure is really helpful in determining the classification of a border pattern. (See page 418.) First note that the classification of every border pattern consists of two symbols. The two symbols are determined as follows:

1. Does the pattern have vertical reflection symmetry? If yes, the first symbol is m (for mirror); if not, the first symbol is 1.
2. Does the pattern have horizontal reflection symmetry? If yes, the second symbol is m, and you are done. If not, proceed to step 3.
3. Does the pattern have glide reflection symmetry? If so, the second symbol is g, and you are done. If not, proceed to step 4.
4. Does the pattern have half-turn symmetry? If so, the second symbol is 2 (for order-2 rotational symmetry) and you are done. If not, proceed to step 5.
5. The second symbol is 1, and you are done.

As for Section 11.6, I have several sheets of complex border patterns that I ask the students to classify, and they seem to find this activity engaging.

A useful resource for Section 11.6 and 11.7 is the free download software *Kali*, available from Jeff Weeks's page: www.geometrygames.org/index.html.

Margaret Morrow, *SUNY Plattsburgh*

Chapter 12
The Mathematics of Fractal Shapes

12.1 The Koch Snowflake
- Self-Similarity
- Perimeter and Area of the Koch Snowflake

12.2 The Sierpinski Gasket

Teaching Tips

Section 12.1

I always start this chapter with a slide show. This consists of about two dozen images and, with discussion, takes up most of the hour, but it is well worth the time. My goal for the slide show is to start some ideas percolating and grease the skids for the more formal concepts discussed in the chapter. As I go through the slides, I ask the students questions such as, "What object is this?" "Is it an object from nature or man-made (art or computer-generated?)" "Is it a close-up or taken from a distance?" Some images are of obvious things (a head of cauliflower and a tree branch), where the level of magnification is not obvious. This is the opening for a discussion on self-similarity in natural shapes. Other images are not at all obvious. Some are taken from space (I use mostly images from the Landsat satellite), others are taken at the microscopic level (I get these from various sources), and others are modern art or computer recreations of natural shapes (I get these mostly on the Internet). The point I try to illustrate with the slides is that there are recurring images in nature that can be found in different objects at many different scales. Another important theme introduced in the slide show is that of an object having "small" volume but "large" surface area (or, in the two-dimensional version, "small" area and "large" perimeter). I have found that starting the chapter with the slide show really helps motivate the students to try to understand the more complicated mathematical ideas that come later in the chapter. At the very least, it gives them a sense of where we are going with the math.

When it comes to the discussion of the perimeter and area of the Koch snowflake, I show that the perimeter is infinite, but skip the exact computation of the area. (I just state that, "after an involved computation—the details are in the textbook—it turns out that the area is 1.6 times (or 60% larger than) the area of the seed triangle." I spend a fair amount of time instead in discussing the metabolic advantages for organisms of having "small" volumes and "large" surface areas. This ties in with the discussion initiated in the slide show.

Peter Tannenbaum, *California State University—Fresno*

Section 12.2

An activity that I use when talking fractals is having students use hexagonal "honeycomb" grid paper and generate Pascal's triangle. Because the numbers in Pascal's triangle become large, it is only important to know if the entry is odd or even. Students quickly catch on that an even plus even is even; an odd plus an even is an odd; and odd plus odd is even. Shading "odd" entries results in a Sierpinski gasket (also called a "Sierpinski triangle"). This is a nice connection to Pascal's triangle, a seemingly unrelated topic. Another variation is to shade the multiples of three, four, etc.

Jeri Hamilton, *Yavapai College*

I cover both the Sierpinski gasket and the Sierpinski carpet (see Exercises 23–26) in class.

Peter Tannenbaum, *California State University—Fresno*

Teaching Tips

Section 12.3

Using one of the Web sites listed in the References at the end of this chapter, have students play the chaos game in class or at home. Then, lead a class discussion about what students learned from the chaos game and what they found most interesting or surprising about it.

Abby Tanenbaum

Section 12.4

I demonstrate the implementation of the "cut" and "twist" steps in the construction of the twisted Sierpinski gasket using GeoGebra (a free dynamic mathematics software package available at www.geogebra.com). I run the program one step at a time for five steps. Then I run the program a second time and show the resulting gaskets side-by-side. This helps the students to visualize the nondeterministric nature of the construction and the notion of "approximate" self-similarity. After this discussion, I show a few slides of mountains (real and computer-generated). The students are asked to guess which is which.

Peter Tannenbaum, *California State University—Fresno*

Section 12.5

It is easy to be seduced and spend an entire week on this section. I spend one class period on the technical part—a minimalist approach to complex numbers and the rest of the class period going over examples of Mandelbrot sequences. I start the second class period with the definition of the *Mandelbrot set* and give a superficial explanation of how the escaping points are assigned colors. This takes about 10–15 minutes. I then reward the students for their patience by spending the rest of the class period showing slides and then video "fly-bys" of the Mandelbrot set. There are many such videos available on YouTube. (Some good ones are listed in the References at the end of the chapter.)

Peter Tannenbaum, *California State University—Fresno*

Chapter 13
Collecting Statistical Data

13.1 The Population
- The *N*-Value

13.2 Sampling
- Public Opinion Polls
- Convenience Sampling
- Quota Sampling

Teaching Tips

Section 13.1

In 2008, most college-age students were too young during the last U.S. Census to remember their parents filling out the forms, so many of them will not be at all familiar with just how the census is conducted. The students seem to enjoy discussing the difficulties with taking a complete census, providing ideas about which parts of the population are likely to be missed. I also discuss some of the controversy about whether more accurate information about the population might be obtained by random sampling. Students do not initially believe that this might be possible, and this nicely sets the stage for discussing random sampling in Section 13.3. The U.S. Census Bureau website (www.census.gov) provides a rich resource for students to explore. You can ask them to research some topic on the site, and write a brief report on it.

Margaret Morrow, *SUNY Plattsburgh*

■ ■ ■

I start with a couple of examples in which statistics are used in a way that is either misleading or somewhat confusing. One example I use is a bar graph showing the percentage of different brands of trucks still on the road after 10 years. The vertical scale runs from 95 to 100%. They easily see how the advertiser is using this to get them to believe that their truck is much better than their competitors, when the actual difference in the percentages between the high and low is less than 2%.

I spend about a day talking about the presidential case studies from the text. These are great examples to illustrate selection and nonresponse bias and also the evolution of sampling techniques.

Deirdre Smith, *University of Arizona*

Section 13.2

I usually give my students a survey question and ask them to discuss how they would get a representative sample of 400 students to answer the question. List all ideas on the board (without commenting on them). Then introduce vocabulary of sampling and point out student-generated examples of each.

MaryAnne Anthony, *Santa Ana College*

■ ■ ■

Teaching Tips

Discuss with the class whether they think the constant barrage of poll results in Presidential elections is a good thing or not. Do they think that voters are influenced in their votes or even in deciding whether to vote by the results of polls? Ask students whether they or a member of their family has ever been polled and whether they agreed to participate in the poll. Discuss what is meant by a "poll of polls."

This section lends itself well to projects. One project idea is to have students examine how well polls taken before the last U.S. Presidential election or presidential primaries predicted the actual results in your state. If this topic is no longer of current interest, polling data from a more recent state or local election could be used instead.

Another project idea is to have students work in groups to conduct their own polls on topics that interest them. Each group should decide on the subject of their poll, design the poll, select an appropriate sample of students at your college, conduct the poll, and analyze the results. Require each group to either submit a written report or report their findings orally to the class, including graphics in the presentation.

Abby Tanenbaum

Section 13.3

My students usually do not initially believe that random sampling is more likely to yield accurate results than sampling based on selecting what one believes to be representative. Many of them believe that the best way to obtain a representative sample would be to have some "informed person" select individuals whom they feel are representative. I find it essential to have some kind of hands-on demonstration of the efficacy of random sampling. I use the random rectangle sheet from *Activity-Based Statistics* by Richard L. Scheaffer, Mrudulla Gnanadesikan, Ann Watkins, and Jeffrey A. Witmer, published by Key Curriculum Press. The sheet shows 100 rectangles with different areas, drawn on quad paper, and numbered from 1 to 100. (Area is measured simply as a number of squares.) The idea is to explore the average area of rectangles in randomly selected samples of size 5.

Random samples can be obtained by using calculators to generate random numbers, or one can simply use a random number table to draw random samples. (An Internet search for "random number table" provides several examples.) To use a random number table to identify rectangles, one should decide which two digits of the numbers on the table will be used to identify the rectangles. One then begins anywhere in the table, recording the two digits selected. One then moves in any direction in the table, skipping any number of numbers before reading off the next pair of digits, provided only that one repeats this consistently. Repeat until one has obtained the required number of randomly chosen numbers between 1 and 100. (Note: Interpret 00 as 100, consider 01 as 1, and so on.) It can happen that the same rectangle shows up twice in a sample of 5. If students ask about this, tell them to discard the second appearance of the rectangle, and select another rectangle for the sample.

Margaret Morrow, *SUNY Plattsburgh*

13.3 Random Sampling

- Simple Random Sampling
- Stratified Sampling

Teaching Tips

Section 13.4

Following up on our work in Section 13.3, once the students have been convinced of the efficacy of random sampling, we discuss ways in which one might be biased if one tries to "select" a representative sample using one's best judgment. The small rectangles that one does not notice in the random rectangle experiment provide a good analogy for the less noticeable members of society. Again students seem to enjoy suggesting ways in which observers might be biased.

You can ask students to write about an opinion poll of their choice that is based on a sample they strongly suspect is biased. (They come up with polls based on free-response via the Internet, telephone, etc.)

Margaret Morrow, *SUNY Plattsburgh*

Section 13.5

Begin this section with a quick review of the concepts of a *ratio* and a *proportion*. Review the steps for solving a proportion. Give them some practice on solving simple proportions. Students may suggest *cross multiplication*. Explain what this means and why it works.

Instead of using the approximation "equation" $N \approx \frac{n_1 \cdot n_2}{k}$ given in the text, some students may prefer to solve capture-recapture problems by writing out the proportion

$$\frac{k}{n_2} = \frac{n_1}{N}$$

and substituting the values for n_1, n_2, and k and solving the proportion for N, understanding that the result will be an *approximate* value for N. Although this approach is equivalent to the presentation in the text, it will be more familiar to students based on previous their previous work with proportions.

Abby Tanenbaum

Section 13.6

If you live near an academic medical center, see if you can obtain a guest speaker to talk about clinical trials that have been conducted recently or are currently being conducted at that institution.

Ask students to bring in articles from newspapers, magazines, or the Internet about the results of studies that were based on clinical trials.

Discuss how clinical trials might be biased. Many drug trials are funded by the pharmaceutical companies. Ask students how this might bias the trials and the reported results.

Abby Tanenbaum

Teaching Tips

Section 14.1

Students start to realize how important a frequency table is for organizing a lot of data when they see all the scores given in Table 14-1. Even though the frequency tables in this section are shown by rows, I also make up an example of how a frequency table looks organized by columns, with the frequency always the second column.

Margaret Michener, *University of Nebraska at Kearney*

■ ■ ■

I spend a little bit of time talking about the different graphical representations of data. For the most part, I find that students are familiar with this material. Instead of spending lots of class time on this, I give students an assignment that walks them through how to do this graphing on a spreadsheet. I give them an example of quiz scores and walk them through making a bar graph of this information. Then, when we are discussing Section 14.2, I ask them to come up with three of their own (different) examples that would be represented by a bar graph, a histogram, and a pie chart.

Deirdre Smith, *University of Arizona*

Section 14.2

I put some formulas on the board that students can write in their notes to help them with this section. They are:

$$\% = \frac{\text{frequency}}{N}$$

$$\text{actual frequency} = \% \times N.$$

For angle measure when creating pie charts, use the proportion

$$\frac{\%}{100} = \frac{\text{degrees}}{360}$$

and cross multiply. I like the last formula because it works both for finding degrees if you know the percent, and vice versa.

One thing students may have trouble with understanding at first is the endpoint convention for class intervals, so you may need to spend extra time on this.

Margaret Michener, *University of Nebraska at Kearney*

■ ■ ■

Explain, iterate, and reiterate the importance of sorting a data set prior to any calculations. Failing to do so is a very common mistake.

Ryan Sieve, *University of Kansas*

Section 14.3

I like to show examples with outliers that skew the mean, but not the median. Keep reminding students that numbers must be sorted first from minimum to maximum before the median and quartiles can be found. Also, since some calculators can figure these calculations automatically but the answers may vary from the book, I only give credit for problems done by hand.

Margaret Michener, *University of Nebraska at Kearney*

■ ■ ■

Chapter 14
Descriptive Statistics

14.1 General Descriptions of Data

- Data Sets
- Bar Graphs and Variations Thereof

14.2 Variables

- Class Intervals
- Histograms

14.3 Numerical Summaries of Data

- The Mean (Average)
- Percentiles
- The Median and the Quartiles
- The Five-Number Summary
- Box Plots

14.4 Measures of Spread

- The Range
- The Interquartile Range
- The Standard Deviation

Teaching Tips

Explain each placeholder as minimum, 1st quartile, median, 3rd quartile, and max and their role in the data set. Do not try to explain a box-and-whisker plot simultaneously. It is best to build their vocabulary and understanding of the breakdown of the data and then give a visual representation.

Ryan Sieve, *University of Kansas*

Section 14.4

I ask the students to create a data set with $n = 5$, mean $=$ median $= 70$. I put several of their data sets on the board, and then we discuss the differences between them. This leads to the definitions of *range*, *standard deviation*, and *variance*.

MaryAnne Anthony, *Santa Ana College*

■ ■ ■

Again, work must be shown the way the book explains standard deviation for credit. When students work standard deviation by hand, they get the idea of what they are actually finding. This works well when working problems that have the same mean, but the numbers become more spread out, as some of the exercises in the book show.

Margaret Michener, *University of Nebraska at Kearney*

■ ■ ■

After completing Chapters 13 and 14, I spend a day on creative ways to present statistics and misuses of statistics. I tell students when we start the chapters on statistics to start looking for examples of both creative ways to present statistics graphically and ways to mislead people using statistics. If I have a computer in the classroom, I will take them to the *USA Today* snapshots website: www.usatoday.com/news/snapshot.htm. *USA Today* has daily wonderful examples of creative bar graphs. I also have collected several examples throughout the years. I ask students to bring in these examples and present them to the class. They are required to neatly cut out the example and to paste the example to a pieces of paper and to write out why they think the example is creative for the first assignment and misleading for the second. I have gotten some great examples (and ones I use in class) from my students.

Deirdre Smith, *University of Arizona*

■ ■ ■

Clearly explain how standard deviation and variance are related. Most students do not understand the difference.

Ryan Sieve, *University of Kansas*

Chapter 15

Chances, Probabilities, and Odds

15.1 Random Experiments and Sample Spaces

15.2 Counting Outcomes in Sample Spaces

15.3 Permutations and Combinations

Teaching Tips

Section 15.1

Writing the sample space can be laborious. Encourage tree diagrams instead of listing outcomes.

Tejinder S. Neelon, *California State University San Marcos*

Section 15.2

I have some children's valentines that show three people, each "cut" into head, body, and feet, and have students find out how many different "people" can be formed. This leads to the multiplication rule. (Any manipulatives will work, but it's best if you find something that allows repetition.) Then I show students an old menu from an Italian restaurant with choices of pasta, choices of sauce, and choices of soup or salad. We apply the multiplication rule to figure out the number of different meals that can be ordered from this menu.

MaryAnne Anthony, *Santa Ana College*

■ ■ ■

Students usually remember most of their basic probability facts. We spend some time here discussing sample spaces for cards, rolling two dice, and flipping coins. Students write down the sample spaces for these items to use throughout the rest of the chapter.

Molly L. Beauchman, *Yavapai College*

■ ■ ■

Tree diagram representation also makes counting easier.

Tejinder S. Neelon, *California State University San Marcos*

Section 15.3

The difference between permutations and combinations is a difficult concept for students. Use the analogy of straight poker vs. five-card stud.

Tejinder S. Neelon, *California State University San Marcos*

■ ■ ■

Many students have trouble distinguishing between permutations and combinations, so spend time discussing the differences between them. However, some students will be able to verbalize the differences and yet still have trouble knowing which one to apply to a particular problem. The more "mixed practice" they can do involving the multiplication rule, permutations, and combinations, the better.

Abby Tanenbaum

Teaching Tips

Section 15.4

I start the discussion of probability by actually conducting an experiment. I put my students in groups of two and have them flip a coin 50 times and record the results. It seems a little childish, but they really enjoy it. Once everyone has finished, I write down all of the results and we calculate P(heads) for each group. Not everyone ends up with the probability being $\frac{1}{2}$. We then discuss why this is the case.

LaRonda Oxendine, Robeson Community College

Section 15.5

Some examples of experiments with outcomes that are *not* equiprobable are tossing a thumbtack and tossing a coin with gum on one side.

Tejinder S. Neelon, *California State University San Marcos*

Section 15.6

Emphasize the difference between the use of a fraction such as $\frac{3}{4}$ to express as odds vs. to express a probability.

Tejinder S. Neelon, *California State University San Marcos*

Teaching Tips

Section 16.1

The data from the rectangle experiment suggested for Section 13.3 provide a histogram that is approximately normal. There are also some very good online applets to illustrate that sampling distributions are approximately normal; see

http://www.ruf.rice.edu/~lane/stat_sim/sampling_dist/

(for distribution of sample means) and

http://statweb.calpoly.edu/chance/applets/Reeses/ReesesPieces.html

(for distribution of sample proportions). I found that I needed to explain very carefully what these were showing when demonstrating them to the class.

Margaret Morrow, SUNY Plattsburgh

Section 16.2

I do this section without having covered Section 14.3 in depth. I find I can fairly quickly teach students what they need to know about means, medians, quartiles and standard deviations to make sense of this section.

Margaret Morrow, SUNY Plattsburgh

Section 16.3

Do not underestimate the difficulty that some students have in using their calculators to perform these calculations. I find it helpful in this kind of situation to give the students an example to calculate and then circulate among those who do not get the correct answer to help them figure out where they are going wrong in their calculator usage. Also, do not underestimate how difficult students find it to go back from z-values to x-values, as in Example 16.6.

Margaret Morrow, SUNY Plattsburgh

Section 16.4

I think that the 68-95-99.7 rule is a really useful rule of thumb for students to take with them from the course, and so I stress this section and the next one.

Several students may have come across the use of tables to calculate probabilities with normal curves, or might do so in them future. To help them relate the 68-95-99.7 rule to this, I briefly show them the applet at http://members.shaw.ca/ron.blond/TLE/norm.APPLET/index.html.

Margaret Morrow, SUNY Plattsburgh

Chapter 16
The Mathematics of Normal Distributions

16.1 Approximately Normal Distributions of Data

16.2 Normal Curves and Normal Distributions

16.3 Standardizing Normal Data

16.4 The 68-95-99.7 Rule

Teaching Tips

Section 16.5

The important points to emphasize are:
1. Areas of regions under the normal curve correspond to percentages of the population with scores in the corresponding interval on the x-axis, and the percentage corresponding to the *whole* area under the curve is 100%.
2. Those percentages correspond to the probabilities that a randomly chosen member of the population will have a score lying in the corresponding interval on the x-axis.

I find that with an appropriate in-class worksheet, student fairly quickly understand how to piece together areas under the normal curve to successfully answer questions such as Exercises 45–48. I insist that the students draw simple sketches of normal curves and shade appropriate areas when doing these kinds of problems. When teaching this, I take care to have different students show different methods for calculating the percentage of area in a given region, and stress that there are many correct ways of reaching the answer.

Margaret Morrow, *SUNY Plattsburgh*

Section 16.6

The applet http://statweb.calpoly.edu/chance/applets/Reeses/ReesesPieces.html mentioned in the teaching tips for Section 16.1 also provides a good demonstration for this section.

Margaret Morrow, *SUNY Plattsburgh*

Section 16.7

I emphasize the application of the principles to confidence intervals for opinion polls. (See Example 16.13.) This is particularly relevant in election years! Students said they found it interesting to really understand the mathematics behind the opinion polls reported in the media. (Most such polls are based on a 95% confidence interval.) I tell the students that before they take opinion polls mentioned in the media seriously, they should explore the sampling methods used, and in particular determine how large the sample was.

The Gallup website exemplifies good reporting of opinion polls. I have my students read and report on some of the articles on this site: www.gallup.com. In particular, I ask them to note the careful reporting in these articles of details about when and how the sample was obtained, and the sample size.

Margaret Morrow, *SUNY Plattsburgh*

AVAILABLE PRINT AND MEDIA SUPPLEMENTS

Student Supplements	Instructor Supplements

Student Resource Guide

- By Dale R. Buske, *St. Cloud State University*
- Contains worked-out solutions to odd-numbered exercises from the text
- Includes "selected hints" that point the reader in one of many directions leading to a solution
- Contains keys to student success, including lists of skills that will help prepare for the chapter exams.

ISBNs: 978-0-321-57519-7 and 0-321-57519-9

Videos on DVD with Optional Subtitles

- DVD format enables students to watch the videos at home or on campus
- Feature engaging chapter summaries and examples solutions
- Format provides distance-learning students with critical video instruction of each chapter, but also allows students needing only small amounts of review to watch instruction on a specific problem type
- Include optional subtitles that can be turned off or on for individual student needs

ISBN: 978-0-321-57522-7 and 0-321-57522-9

NEW! Instructor's Edition

- This special edition of the text includes answers to all walking and jogging exercises in a separate section in the back of the book.

ISBNs: 978-0-321-56508-2 and 0-3321-56508-8

Instructor's Solutions Manual

- By Dale R. Buske, *St. Cloud State University*
- Contains solutions to all the exercises in the text

ISBNs: 978-0-321-57516-6 and 0-321-57516-4

Instructor's Testing Manual (download only)

- By Joseph P. Kudrle, *University of Vermont*
- This manual includes four alternative tests per chapter. Two have multiple-choice exercises, and two have free-response exercises.

  Available for download from www.pearsonhighered.com/irc.

NEW! Insider's Guide

- Includes resources to help faculty with course preparation and classroom management.
- Provides helpful teaching tips correlated to each section of the text, as well as general teaching advice and additional resources for classroom enrichment

ISBNs: 978-0-321-57620-0 and 0-321-57620-9

PowerPoint® Lecture Slides (download only)

- Available through www.pearsonhighered.com/irc or inside your MyMathLab online course, these classroom presentations cover all important topics from the text.

	Instructor Supplements
	TestGen® (download only)
	• Enables instructors to build, edit, print, and administer tests using a computerized bank of questions that cover all the objectives of the text
	• Using algorithmically based questions, allows instructors to create multiple but equivalent versions of the same questions or test with the click of a button
	• Lets instructors to modify test bank questions or add new questions
	• Provides printable or online tests
	• Software and testbank available for download through www.pearsonhighered.com/irc or inside your MyMathLab course
	Pearson Math Adjunct Support Center
	(www.pearsontutorservices.com/math-adjunct.html) is staffed by qualified instructors with more than 50 years of combined experience at both the community college and university level. Assistance is provided for faculty in the following areas:
	• Suggested syllabus consultation
	• Tips on using materials bundled with your book
	• Book-specific content assistance
	• Teaching suggestions, including advice on classroom strategies

Getting Started with MathXL®

Overview

MathXL is a powerful online homework, tutorial, and assessment system tied to Pearson Education textbooks in Mathematics and Statistics. Ideal for use in a lecture, self-paced, or distance-learning course, MathXL diagnoses students' weaknesses and creates a personalized study plan based on their test results. MathXL provides students with unlimited practice using a database of algorithmically-generated exercises correlated to the exercises in their textbook. Each tutorial exercise is accompanied by an interactive guided solution and a sample problem to help students improve their skills independently. Instructors can use MathXL to create online homework assignments, quizzes, and tests that are automatically graded and tracked. Instructors can view and manage all students' homework and test results, study plans, and tutorial work in MathXL's flexible online gradebook.

How to Adopt MathXL

1. Getting Access

If you are interested in using MathXL for one or more of your courses, contact your Pearson Education sales representative to request a *MathXL Instructor Access Kit*. (If you are not sure who your sales representative is, go to http://www.pearsonhighered.com/educator/replocator/.) The access kit provides you with an **instructor access code** for registration.

2. Registering

Registering is an easy process that takes only a few minutes, and you need to register only once, even if you are teaching more than one course with MathXL. Detailed instructions are included in the instructor access kit. As part of the registration process, you select a login name and password that you will use from then on to access your MathXL course. Once you have your instructor access code, go to www.mathxl.com, click the **Register** button, and follow the on-screen instructions to register and log in.

3. Creating Your MathXL Course

Once you've registered, creating your MathXL course is easy! Simply log in at www.mathxl.com, go to the Course Manager, and click "Create or copy a course". You will be asked to select the textbook you are using and enter some very basic information about your course. You can create as many courses as you need, and you can customize course coverage to match your syllabus if you wish.

4. Ordering Books for Your Students

To access your MathXL course, each student needs to register in MathXL using a student access code. The easiest way to supply your students with access codes is to order your textbook packaged with the *MathXL Student Access Kit*. Visit the **Books Available** section of the website at www.mathxl.com for a complete list of package ISBNs.

How to Learn More about MathXL

- To learn more about MathXL, visit our website at www.mathxl.com, or contact your Pearson Education sales representative to schedule a demonstration.
- For detailed instructions on how to register, log in, and set up your first MathXL course, visit the **Getting Started** section of the MathXL website at www.mathxl.com.

Powered by CourseCompass™ and MathXL®

Getting Started with MyMathLab®

Overview

MyMathLab is a series of text-specific online courses that accompany Pearson Education textbooks in Mathematics and Statistics. Since 2001, MyMathLab has helped over 3 million students succeed at math at more than 1,750 colleges and universities. Students and educators alike have benefited from MyMathLab's dependable and easy-to-use online homework, tests, guided solutions, multimedia, ebooks, and tutorial exercises. Pearson's service teams provide training and support when you need it, and MyMathLab offers the broadest range of titles available for adoption.

When you adopt the MyMathLab course for your textbook, your students can view the textbook pages in electronic form and link to supplemental multimedia resources—such as animations and video clips—directly from the eBook. MyMathLab provides students with algorithmically-generated tutorial exercises correlated to the exercises in their text, and the system generates individualized study plans based on student test results. MyMathLab's powerful homework and test managers and flexible online gradebook make it easy for instructors to create and manage online assignments that are automatically graded, so they can spend less time grading and more time teaching!

How to Adopt MyMathLab

1. **Getting Access**

   If you are interested in using MyMathLab for one or more of your courses, contact your Pearson Education sales representative to request a *MyMathLab Instructor Access Kit*. (If you are not sure who your sales representative is, go to http://www.pearsonhighered.com/educator/replocator/.) The access kit provides you with an **instructor access code** for registration.

2. **Registering**

   MyMathLab courses are accessed through an online learning environment called CourseCompass, so to adopt a MyMathLab course, you need to register in CourseCompass. Registering is an easy process that takes only a few minutes, and you need to register only once, even if you are teaching more than one MyMathLab course. As part of the registration process, you select a login name and password that you will use from then on to access your MyMathLab course. Once you have your instructor access code, go to www.coursecompass.com, click the **Register** button for educators, and follow the on-screen instructions to register and log in.

3. **Creating Your MyMathLab Course**

   Once you've registered in CourseCompass, creating your MyMathLab course is easy. You will simply be asked to select the course materials for your textbook and enter some very basic information about your course. Approximately one business day later (and often after only an hour or two), you will be notified via e-mail that your course is ready, and you will then be able to log in and begin exploring MyMathLab.

4. **Ordering Books for Your Students**

   To access your MyMathLab course, each student needs to register in CourseCompass using a student access code. The easiest way to supply your students with access codes is to order your textbook packaged with the *MyMathLab Student Access Kit*. Visit the **Books Available** section of the website at www.mymathlab.com for a complete list of package ISBNs.

How to Learn More about MyMathLab

- To learn more about MyMathLab, visit our website at www.mymathlab.com, or contact your Pearson Education sales representative to schedule a demonstration.
- For detailed instructions on how to register, log in, and set up your first MyMathLab course, visit the **Getting Started** section of the MyMathLab website at www.mymathlab.com.

HELPFUL TIPS FOR USING SUPPLEMENTS AND TECHNOLOGY

Molly L. Beauchman, *Yavapai College*

■ MyMathLab: I use MyMathLab for homework assignments and for practice tests.

MyMathLab Homework: Homework assignments have specific due dates, and students can submit the assignment as many times as they would like before the due date. I use this as successful practice. Students can also print the problem(s) they are having trouble with and we will discuss them in class. Homework is 15% of the course grade.

MyMathLab Practice Tests: Practice tests are available for students, but not graded. Tests are given in class that are similar to the practice tests.

MyMathLabTests: I create tests for my online students using the problems available in MyMathLab. Students can only take these once and they are timed. There is also a written component of each chapter test that includes an extended real life application of the content in the chapter.

MyMathLab Videos: If students miss class, I encourage them to view the lecture videos.

■ Other Videos: I also make my own videos for each section of the text for my online course and make these available for my in-class students. These videos focus on the content students have difficulty with and contain directions for how to use technology— graphing calculators and *Excel* or another spreadsheet program.

Norma Biscula, *University of Maine, Augusta*

■ If possible, schedule the second or third class in a computer lab to insure that all students are able to log onto MyMathLab (MML). MyMathLab has proven to be an excellent support tool for those students who invest the time required to learn how to use the program. Make sure to point out the announcement that links to the <u>How to Enter</u> <u>Answers Using the MathXL Player</u> tour. If possible, allow students to take the tour in class. Many students become frustrated with MyMathLab due to solution formatting. Taking the tour will help to alleviate many of those problems. I recommend that an extra-credit online quiz be given that asks the students to navigate through the MML program.

■ The appropriate use of technology should be emphasized throughout the course. The majority of students enter the classroom with fairly good graphing calculator skills and acceptable computer skills. For the few students with no prior knowledge of the calculator, the video technicians and I produced a video that shows general operational procedures. The first item presented on the video is how to turn the calculator on and off and the second item is how to return the calculator to machine settings. Video vignettes have been inserted into the course. These vignettes will provide problem specific and technology tutorials. Students who lack computer skills are asked to attend basic workshops that are offered through the computer services department. Lastly, I strongly recommend the use of Tablet PCs in all mathematics class. My students rated the Tablet as their preferred method of delivery.

Rosemary Danaher, *Sacred Heart University*

■ I use MyMathLab for all courses I teach, and consider it a very valuable tool. I assign exercises for each unit I cover in the textbook. In addition, I assign written project work apart from MyMathLab. I consider the primary benefits of MyMathLab to be the following:

1. Online Help: Students who cannot solve a problem can select this feature. The software will then assist the student in solving the problem, in a step-by-step approach. In addition, the software will allow the student to work on similar problems to reinforce the concept.

2. "Ask My Instructor": If the student wants to interact with me on a particular exercise, they can select this feature. The student will key-in their questions/concerns and an e-mail is then sent to the instructor. The e-mail includes a link to the exact exercise so that I can actually view the details and comment back via e-mail. This is a very timely feature, as my students are often working on homework at night. I check my e-mails at approximately 9:30 P.M. and respond that evening so students are not delayed in completing their assignments.

3. "Similar Exercise": If a student is having difficulty with a particular exercise or just wants more practice, the software allows him or her to select this option and work on additional problems.

4. Random Generator: The software ensures the problems are somewhat random by varying the numeric values associated with the problem. This helps, but does not totally eliminate the possibility of students copying each other's work.

5. Due Dates: The instructor can assign due dates to assignments, ensuring students do not wait until the end of the semester to complete the work.

6. Edit capability of assignments: While you can automatically assign a complete unit for students to complete, I do not recommend this approach because I have found in some rare instances problems were included in a unit that were not relevant to the material covered. Just as important, I feel the instructor should be familiar with each of the problems assigned, which requires that you review the exercises first. A nice feature of the software is that you can selectively include or exclude exercises.

7. Online grading of assignments: The software grades each assignment when the student submits his or her work. This frees up the instructor to focus on lecture preparation and other project work. I believe the biggest complaint I had from students was concerning multiple-part questions. If a student's answer to one part of the exercise was incorrect, the software would mark the entire exercise wrong.

Jeri Hamilton, *Yavapai College*

■ I make assignments on MyMathLab weekly. Generally I will post an assignment on Monday and have the assignment due on the following Monday by midnight. I allow students to work through the homework as many times in that week as possible with no time limit other than they have to complete the assignment before the Monday deadline. I think that they feel more at ease knowing that they could feasibly work hard to get 100% on each assignment if they wished. Usually on the first or second day of class, I spend a lot of time demonstrating how to use MyMathLab and the multimedia supplements available to the students.

LaRonda Oxendine, *Robeson Community College*

■ I use the PowerPoint presentations provided for each chapter as part of my lecture. (I just download them from MyMathLab.)

■ I make the video lectures available in the office area for my students.

■ Over the years, I have realized that students will not complete the assigned homework unless it is graded. Since the online homework component of MyMathLab is such a great tool, I am going to require my students to complete an online homework assignment for each chapter.

Useful Classroom Resources For Teachers

Provided by:

Mary Anne Anthony, *Santa Ana College*

Molly L. Beauchman, *Yavapai College*

Norma Biscula, *University of Maine, Augusta*

Alicia Gordon, *Meredith College*

Jeri Hamilton, *Yavapai College*

Kathleen Offenholley, *Brookdale Community College*

LaRonda Oxendine, *Robeson Community College*

Linda Padilla, *Joliet Junior College*

Graph Theory Project
Chapter 5–7

Chapter 5: The Königsberg Bridge Problem

1. Draw a graph of the town of Königsberg. Add or subtract as many bridges as you like until you have a graph where you can go over every bridge exactly once. *Write the degree next to each vertex.*

2. Discuss with your group various other maps of Königsberg that also work. Draw three of those graphs here. *Write the degree next to each vertex.*

3. How many even vertices does each graph above have? List them here.

4. Are there any graphs where you can start at one spot in town, cross over each bridge exactly once, and *return to the start*? How many even and how many odd vertices do those graphs have?

5. In the original map of Königsberg, in which you *cannot* cross every bridge exactly once, how many odd vertices do you have? How many even vertices?

6. In your group, make a guess as to what pattern of even and odd vertices allows you to be able to cross each bridge exactly once, or to be able to cross each bridge once and come back to the start.

Use a graph to determine whether there is a path through these rooms that goes through every doorway exactly once.

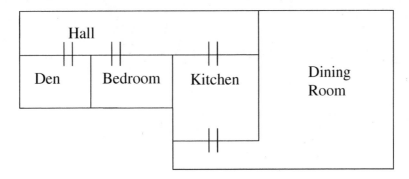

1. Draw the graph. *Each room should be a vertex. Each door corresponds to an edge.*
   (If there are two doors that lead from one room to another, there should be two edges;
   every door should be represented by an edge.)

2. Write the degree of each vertex *on the graph.*

3. If there is a path through the rooms that goes through every doorway exactly once, state
   what the path would be.

4. Explain how you know whether or not there is a path *using Euler's path theorem.*

5. Is there a path through the rooms that goes through every doorway exactly once and back
   to the room in which you started? Explain how you know.

Chapter 6: Hamilton Circuits

Choose four states or countries to which you would like to travel. Use an atlas, a newspaper, or an online travel site for your research. Created a weighted graph of these places *and your own* state that shows *either*

a) the number of miles between each state and every other states *or*
b) the cost of an airplane (or if you prefer, train or bus) ticket from every place to every other.

Your graph should be a complete, weighted graph with five vertices, including your own state.

1. Draw the graph here. (Remember that it's OK for lines to cross, but be as neat as possible.)

2. Use the *nearest-neighbor algorithm* to find the approximately cheapest or shortest way to start from home, visit each place, and *return home*. Draw the circuit here.

3. *Explain* how you used the nearest-neighbor algorithm to find the cheapest way. What vertex did you go to first, and why? Second? Third? Why?

4. Using the correct formula, how many Hamilton circuits are in your graph? Show your work.

5. Use the *brute-force algorithm* to find the exact cheapest or shortest way. Use your answer to Question 4 to help you know how many circuits to list.

6. How far off was your approximate (nearest-neighbor) answer compared to the brute-force algorithm?

7. Find out results from the other groups. Were any of their nearest-neighbor answers the same as the brute-force algorithm? Far off? Close?

8. Which algorithm would you want to use if you had to do this problem for your work or to plan a vacation? Why?

Chapter 7: Minimum-Cost Spanning Tree

The following people have each bought mainframe computers in order to create a network. The numbers on each edge represent the miles from one computer to another, so that the group can decide which computers should be connected to which. Not all mileages are given because some computer connections would be impossible (too difficult to connect because access is blocked by a river, a major highway, etc.). Some mileages are quite long because the cable would have to snake around landmarks and buildings.

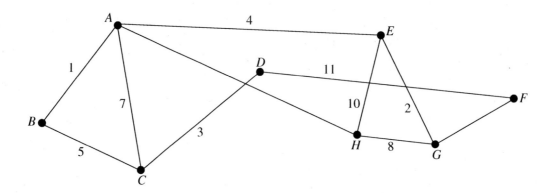

1. Here, or on a separate piece of paper, create a minimal spanning tree so that all the computers are connected in the cheapest way possible (least miles). Please label each vertex of your minimal spanning tree.

2. Using the minimal spanning tree, find the total number of miles of cable you have to put down.

3. When you send an e-mail, it makes many "jumps" from one mainframe computer to another. Use your minimal spanning tree to determine how many miles an e-mail from Delbert (D) to Filomena (F) would have to travel.

4. E-mail often travels in a roundabout way to get from one computer to another. In the original graph, would there have been a way for an e-mail to get from Delbert (D) to Filomena (F) in fewer jumps, or in fewer miles?

5. Why was that path eliminated from the minimal spanning tree?

Graph Theory Project
ANSWER KEY

The Königsberg Bridge Problem
1–3. Answers will vary, but should have two odd vertices, the rest even, or all even vertices.
4. To be able to return to the start, each vertex must be even.
5. In the original map of Königsberg, all the vertices are odd.
6. Any reasonable guesses are fine here, to prepare students for Section 14.2.

Using Euler's Path Theorem
1. and 2. Graphs may vary in how they look, but should have degrees as follows:
Hall, 4; Den, 1; Bedroom, 1; Kitchen, 2; Dining Room, 2.
3. Paths will start in the den and end in the bedroom, or vice versa.
4. We know there is a path because there are exactly two odd vertices.
5. There a no path through the rooms that goes through every doorway exactly once and back to the room in which you started. We know because that would be an Euler circuit, which much have all even vertices.

Hamilton Circuits
1. Graphs will vary based on the states or countries and price.
2. and 3. Students should go from cheapest or shortest route to next cheapest or shortest.
4. There should be $(5 - 1)! = 4! = 24$ Hamilton circuits.
5. The brute-force method should list all 24 circuits and prices. A quick check that they are probably doing it correctly is that each price will be duplicated. (12 of the circuits will be the same as 12 other circuits.)
6. and 7. Sometimes the nearest neighbor and brute force are the same; most of the time the nearest neighbor is slightly off, since it is only an approximation.
8. Answers will vary (personal opinion).

Minimum-Cost Spanning Tree
1.

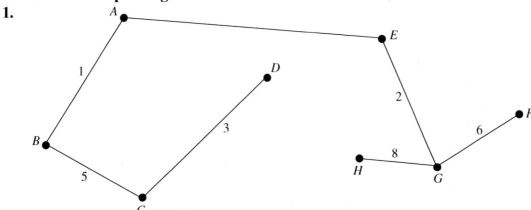

2. Total: 29 miles
3. 21 miles
4. It would have been done in 11 miles. That path was eliminated from the minimal spanning tree because it created a loop and was one of the longest edges.

Project: Hamilton Circuits
Chapter 6

1. Determine four places that you would like to go on an errand day. Count "home" as your *fifth* location.

2. Find the distance in minutes between each location. You can do this by going on the web to a map program such as Yahoo!® Maps, MapQuest®, or Google™ Maps. Create a table showing this information. Tip: The end result is usually "easier" if each leg has a different time. If you don't agree with the map program, use your best guess.

3. Create a network representing this information, including the distances in minutes. This may be drawn by hand or made on the computer, but it should be neat.

4. Apply the **brute-force algorithm** to find the optimal Hamilton Circuit. List all of the circuits you find and their total times. Rewrite your optimal answer starting from "home," listing the total time as well.

5. Apply the **repetitive nearest-neighbor algorithm** to find a Hamilton Circuit. List the five circuits you find and their total times. Rewrite your optimal answer starting from "home," listing the total time as well.

6. Apply the **cheapest-link algorithm** to find a Hamilton Circuit. Rewrite your optimal answer starting from "home," listing the total time as well.

7. Find the percentage difference between your brute-force total (the definite best) and the total you found from the repetitive nearest-neighbor algorithm (your answer from #5 above).

8. Find the percentage difference between your brute-force total (the definite best) and the total you found from the cheapest-link algorithm (your answer from #6 above).

9. Any conclusion? While brute force got you the shortest route, was it worth it?

Grading

Mileage Chart	3 points
Graph	3 points
Overall Presentation and Organization	3 points
Brute-Force Algorithm	5 points
Repetitive Nearest-Neighbor Algorithm	4 points
Cheapest-Link Algorithm	3 points
Percentage Differences	2 points
Conclusion	2 points
Total	**25 points**

Note: You may do this project individually or in pairs. If you are in pairs, you and your partner will receive the same grade.

Mathematics of Rabbit Breeding
Section 9.1

A pair of newly born rabbits, male and female, was placed in a hutch. In two months, these rabbits began their breeding cycle and produced one pair of rabbits, one male and one female. The original rabbits and their offspring continued to breed in this manner, that is, the first pair of offspring appearing at the parental age of two months and then produced a new pair of offspring every month thereafter, always one male and one female. All rabbits survived the first year.

What then is the total number of pairs of rabbits at the beginning of each month during the first year?

MONTH	PAIRS OF RABBITS		
Beginning of	Productive	Nonproductive	Total
1st			
2nd			
3rd			
4th			
5th			
6th			
7th			
8th			
9th			
10th			
11th			
12th			

Answer Key for Rabbit Breeding Activity

MONTH	PAIRS OF RABBITS		
Beginning of	Productive	Nonproductive	Total
1st	0	1	1
2nd	1	0	1
3rd	1	1	2
4th	2	1	3
5th	3	2	5
6th	5	3	8
7th	8	5	13
8th	13	8	21
9th	21	13	34
10th	34	21	55
11th	55	34	89
12th	89	55	144

Applications of Exponential Growth
Section 10.3 and Mini-Excursion 3

Population Growth: The 2000 United States Census counted roughly 281 million people living in the United States at a time when the yearly population growth rate was about 1.2 percent per year. If this rate of growth continues until 2045, what will the population of the United States be then?

Compound Interest: Suppose you deposit $1000 in an account that pays 8% interest per year compounded annually.

a. How much money would be in the account after 5 years?

End of Year:	Amount in the Account
1	
2	
3	
4	
5	

b. Write an equation that models this models this situation.

Loan Project
Section 10.6

Choose one of the following scenarios:
1) Buy a car.
2) Buy a house.
3) Finance your upper division university education through a student loan.

For 1) and 2): Find a car or a house you'd like to purchase. Using the current rate of interest from your bank, a credit union, or another source, calculate the down payment, and then calculate your monthly payments over the life of this purchase. Indicate how much your purchase actually costs you in total and how much of the total cost is interest. Show and explain all your work!

For 3): If you are currently attending a community college and plan to transfer to a four-year school, find out what it costs to attend the college of your choice. Estimate how long it will take you after transferring to earn your bachelor's degree and how much it will cost. Find out what kinds of student loans are available. Then calculate what monthly payments will be required from you, and for how long, to pay back the loan. Finally, calculate the total cost of the loan and how much of it is interest. Show and explain all your work!

$$\$$$

Grading Rubric for Loan Project

Maximum = 50 points

30   Turned-in paper (–1 for each day late)

For purchase of house or car (points):

2   Ad attached, showing item and price
2   Source of financing information
4   Description of loan, including required down payment, length of loan, and rate of interest
3   Correct calculation of down payment and loan principal
3   Correct calculation of amount of each monthly payment
3   Correct calculation of total amount paid for house or car
3   Correct calculation of total interest paid

For student loan (points):

2   Name of university and website giving information about costs
2   Cost per term (semester or quarter?)
2   Reasonable estimate, with rationale, of number of terms needed to earn degree
2   Correct calculation of amount of loan needed
2   Source of financing information
4   Description of loan, including how soon after graduation payments start, when interest starts to accrue, rate of interest, and number of monthly payments
2   Correct calculation of amount of each monthly payment
2   Correct calculation of total amount paid over life of the loan
2   Correct calculation of total interest paid

County Coloring Project
Mini-Excursion 2

To demonstrate that any map can be colored with at most four colors, you will be using the techniques of Mini-Excursion 2 to color a map showing counties in a particular state. Choose one of the states listed below and print out a map showing county lines.

States with 15–24 counties: Arizona, Maine, Nevada, New Jersey, Wyoming, Maryland

One site from which you can get your map: http://www.lib.utexas.edu/maps/county_outline.html

1. Draw a graph model showing the counties as vertices. Connect the counties with edges with those counties that share a common boundary.

2. Develop a coloring scheme based on your graph.

3. Color your map according to your coloring scheme.

4. Turn in your graph and colored map.

STATISTICS PROJECT
Chapters 14 and 16

The following table shows student test grades from a specific course. The fifth space is blank. Please find the class average for each student and place the average in the space provided. Use these averages to answer the questions for your project.

1. a. Find the mean, median, and mode of the following data.

   b. Find the standard deviation.

   c. Make a frequency table of the data with a class width of 5.

   d. Make a histogram of the data.

   e. Does your distribution approximate a normal distribution? Explain your answer.

2. a. Using your knowledge of the score table find the range of grades for the following:

   A = 10%   B = 25%   C = 30%   D = 25%   E = 10%

   b. Compare the results you obtained in 2a with the true percentages. Please explain why or why not the percentages are different.

CLASS GRADES

Student number	Test 1	Test 2	Test 3	Test 4	Average
1	83	78	83	79	
2	98	86	92	97	
3	78	83	64	71	
4	93	95	100	96	
5	71	67	68	58	
6	91	89	97	87	
7	96	86	76	77	
8	80	95	87	95	
9	94	73	68	61	
10	82	78	68	64	
11	67	74	59	75	
12	94	92	100	100	
13	62	60	44	37	
14	75	69	81	80	
15	78	77	76	81	
16	93	93	85	95	
17	92	96	92	88	
18	98	85	99	77	
19	91	92	87	98	
20	77	58	65	63	
21	83	87	77	64	
22	82	72	91	95	
23	85	71	83	64	
24	77	83	78	74	
25	79	96	70	86	
26	96	84	100	83	
27	92	85	82	78	
28	78	66	61	64	
29	94	58	73	74	

Student number	Test 1	Test 2	Test 3	Test 4	Average
30	89	44	80	59	
31	74	87	79	72	
32	67	48	42	56	
33	83	96	86	87	
34	96	100	95	84	
35	100	94	98	97	
36	75	55	75	79	
37	76	58	78	75	
38	90	96	91	94	
39	87	85	72	53	
40	94	96	85	92	
41	66	59	66	60	
42	98	79	52	63	
43	86	86	79	74	
44	92	100	98	100	
45	54	84	74	65	
46	86	68	62	51	
47	84	59	39	42	
48	98	92	71	60	
49	94	93	90	87	
50	77	85	61	82	
51	85	90	75	74	
52	98	100	88	87	
53	79	83	51	65	
54	100	94	98	92	
55	85	86	93	84	
56	84	83	74	83	
57	87	79	54	58	
58	55	56	60	43	
59	67	65	31	38	
60	100	94	98	96	
61	64	44	77	38	
62	100	96	85	97	
63	88	65	71	80	
64	98	86	82	83	
65	67	78	70	65	
66	92	69	76	31	
67	83	64	46	59	
68	100	100	93	92	
69	96	82	56	59	
70	87	74	64	63	
71	94	92	90	82	
72	100	96	92	87	
73	86	96	92	73	
74	95	48	56	43	
75	100	98	94	85	
76	78	56	44	49	
77	98	88	87	86	
78	84	86	76	92	
79	86	84	81	78	

Student number	Test 1	Test 2	Test 3	Test 4	Average
80	78	68	69	75	
81	100	65	56	78	
82	58	49	55	67	
83	97	89	100	71	
84	94	66	76	77	
85	95	58	65	49	
86	100	93	100	97	
87	87	78	76	78	
88	100	96	100	81	
89	94	93	92	93	
90	96	66	64	58	
91	94	94	96	92	
92	95	85	84	77	
93	93	83	88	76	
94	67	76	59	58	
95	88	74	72	78	

Probability Project
Sections 15.4 and 15.5

Choose one of the following projects, or check with me if you have another idea. Your completed project should be 2–4 pages typed or neatly handwritten. If you use any reference materials, be sure to include a bibliography. If you use the Internet as a resource, be sure to include all website addresses you used. Please include this assignment page with your project.

1. Find three examples of how probabilities are used in predicting disasters (natural disasters such as earthquakes and lighting strikes, and other disasters like airplane or automobile crashes). Explain how these probabilities were calculated, and how you use them in planning and making decisions.

2. Research and write a brief report about a genetic disease. Describe, in nontechnical terms, the symptoms and treatment. Include the relative frequency with which this disease is found in the population (in general, or a specific population group) and the probabilities of passing the disease on to the next generation. Be sure to cite the resources you used.

3. Visit the website of the California lottery (www.calottery.com) or any other state lottery and write a report about that lottery. Include the types of games that are available, the cost to play, the prizes awarded, and the probability of winning. Calculate the expected value of one ticket for one of the games. Do you think the lottery is a good way for the state to make money? Why or why not?

Grading Rubric for Probability Project

Maximum = 50 points

30   Turned-in paper (–1 point for each school day late)

Standard grading for all projects (points):

2   Introduction
2   Few or no spelling errors
2   Good grammar
2   Citation of resources used
2   Conclusion

Option 1 (points):

3   Three examples
4   Explanation of how each probability is calculated
3   Explanation of how each is used in planning and making decisions (minimal, moderate, complete)

Option 2 (points):

3   Complete, nontechnical description of genetic disease (minimal, moderate, complete)
2   Includes relative frequency of disease in population
2   Explains whether disease is found in population in general or more specific group
3   Description of how disease is transmitted by heredity (minimal, moderate, complete)

Option 3 (points):

2   Describes games available
2   Gives cost to play each game and prizes awarded
2   States probability of winning each game
2   Calculates correctly the expected value of one ticket
2   Opinion of state raising money from lottery

Heights and the Normal Distribution
Sections 16.3 and 16.4

Are you tall, short, or of average height? Use the 68-95-99.7 rule to answer the following:

The heights of *women* in the United States follow an approximately normal distribution with mean 64 inches and standard deviation 2 inches.

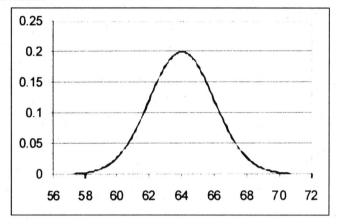

1. What percent of women are between 62 and 66 inches tall?

2. What percent of women are 64 inches or taller?

3. What percent of women are more than 60 inches tall?

4. What percent of women are between 60 and 62 inches tall?

The heights of *men* in the United States follow an approximately normal distribution with mean 69 inches and standard deviation 2.25 inches.

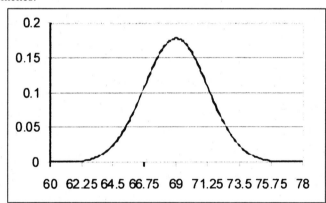

5. What percent of men are between 64.5 and 73.5 inches tall?

6. What percent of men are taller than 71.25 inches?

7. What percent of men are shorter than 66.75 inches?

8. What percent of men are between 62.25 and 71.25 inches tall?

Where do you fit within the distribution of heights for your gender?
Use your calculator to answer the following questions:

9. What percent of the population is shorter than you are?

   What percent of the population is taller than you are?

10. What is your z-value? A z-value standardizes a raw score and shows how many standard deviations a raw score is above or below the mean.

$$z = \frac{x - \mu}{\sigma} = \underline{\hspace{2cm}}$$

11. What percent of the female population is between 63 and 67 inches tall?

12. What is the height that 75% of men are taller than? (Recall from Section 14.3 that this number is called the *75th percentile*.)

13. A female volleyball player at your college is 6 feet 2 inches tall, and a male college soccer player is also 6 feet 2 inches tall. Based on the distribution above, who is taller in relation to the distribution of heights based on gender? Find the z-value for each athlete.

Answer Key for Heights and Normal Distribution Activity

1. 68%

2. 50%

3. 97.5%

4. 13.5%

5. 95%

6. 16%

7. 16%

8. 83.85%

9. Answers will vary.

10. Answers will vary.

11. normalcdf(63, 67, 62, 2) $\approx$ 30.2%

12. invNorm(0.75, 69, 2.25) $\approx$ approximately 70.5 inches

13. Female: $\dfrac{72 - 62}{2} = 5$

    Male: $\dfrac{72 - 69}{2.25} \approx 1.33$

    The female is considered taller in relation to the female population because her height of 72 inches is 5 standard deviations above the mean, while the male height of 72 inches is only 1.33 standard deviations above the mean.

Expected Value (Expectation) Worksheet
Mini-Excursion 4

Assume you are blindfolded and throw a dart at the each of the dart boards shown below.

a) Assuming your dart sticks in the dart board, determine the probabilities that the dart lands on $1, $10, $20, and $100, respectively.

b) If you win the amount of money indicated by the section of the board where the dart lands, find your expectation when you throw the dart.

Board #1

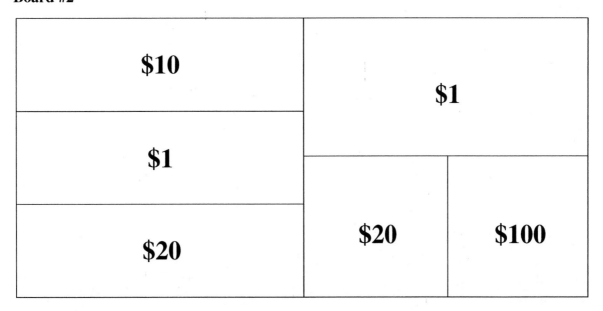

Board #2

Answer Key for Expectation Worksheet

Board #1:

$$P(\$1) = \frac{9}{16}$$

$$P(\$10) = \frac{4}{16} = \frac{1}{4}$$

$$P(\$20) = \frac{2}{16} = \frac{1}{8}$$

$$P(\$100) = \frac{1}{16}$$

$$E = \$11.81$$

Board #2:

$$P(\$1) = \frac{10}{24} = \frac{5}{12}$$

$$P(\$10) = \frac{4}{24} = \frac{1}{6}$$

$$P(\$20) = \frac{7}{24}$$

$$P(\$100) = \frac{3}{24} = \frac{1}{8}$$

$$E = \$20.42$$

HOME-BUYING PROJECT
Section 10.6

Deirdre A. Smith and Debra Wood

University of Arizona

OBJECTIVES:

In this project you will investigate the process of buying a house. For the purposes of this project we will assume that you are going to graduate this semester, get a job, and begin saving for your first house. You will plan to buy your first house five years from now. At that time you will use the money you have saved for the down payment and any closing costs, and then take out a loan for the rest of the cost of the house.

You will do the research for this project in five mini-projects which will be due on the dates given by your instructor. Your instructor will make corrections and suggestions about the contents of the mini-projects and your grade will be counted towards your homework grade. These mini-projects are an extremely important part of this project, as this is the research phase. The feedback you receive will tell you if you are on the right track and will help you write a better final project. You should not, however, just staple these mini-projects together and hand them in for the final project. If you do so, I can guarantee that you will get a low grade on the project.

The following are the 5 mini-projects.

Mini-project 1:

The first step in buying a home is finding a job. Obviously, if you already have a job in your area of study this first mini-project will be easy. If you are not yet employed, remember we are assuming that you will graduate this semester and plan on getting a job. For this project, choose a job that is realistically obtainable with a degree in your major. Of course, you may

want to go to law school or some other graduate school upon graduation, but for this project, just go with the assumption that you plan on entering the workforce immediately upon graduation.

The assignment that you hand in should have the following information:

1. Give the job title and the source of your information. Include the city and state of the job.
2. Provide a job description. This should be at least several sentences long but no longer than one page. This can be in your own words or a cited reference.
3. State the starting salary for the job.
4. Make realistic projections for your salary increases over the next five years. These adjustments should be based either on the salary for an individual in your job with 5 years experience or an adjustment based on inflation. Explain your method of determining each year's salary for the five year period. Be sure to show computations if the increases are given in percent per year raises.

Mini-project 2:

You will need to approximate how much money you can save towards the down payment and closing costs in the next five years. Be realistic. Most people can only save 5-10% of their salary each year. Remember you will need to pay taxes. Every individual must pay federal taxes and Social Security and Medicare taxes. Most people must also pay state taxes (there are some states that do not have state taxes) and some people (generally city dwellers) have local taxes. You will need to find out how much you will be required to pay in taxes (and show all sources and computations) and deduct this amount from your pay.

Do the following for each of the five years you will be saving towards the house:

1. State your yearly and monthly salary for each of the five years.
2. Find the federal, state, local, Social Security, and Medicare taxes that will be deducted from your pay. Be sure to cite your sources and show your computations. If there is no state or local taxes where you intend to live, say so. Do not just neglect to mention a type of taxes.
3. State your yearly and monthly salary after taxes have been deducted. This is your net pay.

Now you need to make up a tentative monthly budget. This should include:

1. Rent. This cannot be a number that you just guess at. If you are currently living in an apartment in the city or town you plan on working in, then you can use this amount. Otherwise, you will need to find an apartment. It should be easy to find a place on the internet. Regardless, you need to cite your sources and, if possible, include a photo or printout of the apartment.
2. Utilities. This should include electric, gas, heat, cable, internet and all phone bills (do not forget to include your cell phone).

3. Food. Be realistic. If you do not know how much you will spend on food, ask your parents or a sibling or friend that lives on their own. Most people spend about $50-100 per week on food. If you go out for a lot of your meals (even fast food) you will likely spend a lot more than this amount.
4. Transportation. This includes car loans, public transportation costs, gasoline, parking, and car maintenance. Even if you currently own your own car outright you will definitely have some repairs and general vehicle maintenance (like new tires and brakes) over the next five years.
5. Insurance. This includes car insurance, renter's insurance, and health insurance. Even though many jobs do pay for a portion of health insurance costs, very few employers pay 100%. Many people also get dental and vision insurance. If you already own a car you can use the rate you currently get (cite source and include a copy of a bill). If you are not currently paying insurance, you need to research insurance rates. I have found

that many students have difficulty finding rates using insurance company websites. To find rates, I think you will have more success talking to an insurance agent. You will need to find several insurance rates while researching this project (besides the ones stated above, you will also need to find homeowner's insurance rates in mini-project 5). If you do end up calling an agent, please read mini-project 4 first so that you know the etiquette appropriate for interaction with any professional you speak to while researching this project.

6. Student loans or any other non-car loans. This would include any large credit card debt.

7. Clothing. Many college students do not consider how much their wardrobe requirements will change upon graduation. There are very few jobs that allow you to dress as you did in college. Even teachers, who are not usually known for their haute couture wardrobe, still need to buy presentable professional clothing.

8. Professional appearance. Haircuts, manicures, toiletries. Even though a tube of toothpaste does not cost a lot, when you consider shampoo, toothpaste, toothbrushes, etc., the cost of these items can add up and do need to be budgeted.

9. Entertainment. We all need to have some social activities. Movies, concerts, going out to dinner, book, magazine, music, DVDs...

10. Miscellaneous expenses. Even though the above list seems rather conclusive, there are a lot of costs in life that are unexpected. Things like vacations, unexpected trips that need to be made (a funeral or wedding), etc. You should allot about 15-20% of your monthly income for miscellaneous expenses.

Subtract this amount from your total net salary for the next five years. For the sake of the project you can assume that the budget costs will stay the same for the next five years (in reality, this probably is not true). This should allow you to compute the amount of money you can save over the next five years.

Mini-project 3:

What will you do with the money you are able to save every month? Invest it, of course. There are many ways to invest money but for the sake of this project, you will invest your savings in a savings account that is safe and predictable.

1. Find a savings account to invest your money in. The interest will probably be rather low, but that is OK. The money you are saving will be going into the account on a monthly basis and you will only have the account for the five years. After the five years, your savings will go towards the down payment and will pay all closing costs. Be sure to document the interest rate you will be earning and the bank you will be depositing your money. It is a good idea to include a print out from the bank showing the interest rate you will be getting.

2. Use the amount of money you are saving each month, the interest rate you found, and your knowledge of annuities to compute how much money you will have after 5 years. Do not forget to include the formulas you use. Now is a good time to start compiling a list of all the formulas you will be using for the final project.

Mini-project 4:

Now that you know how much money you have for a down payment and closing costs, you need to start researching the home you plan to buy. First, start with the Affordability Guidelines in the text to decide upon a price range. The best place to start is with Affordability Guideline #1, which states that the house you can afford should be no more than 3 times your annual salary. Remember this guideline assumes that you will have a 20% down payment. If you do not have 20% in savings, this does not mean that you cannot afford a home – it just means that you probably need to go down a little with the price of your house. After you finish mini-project 5 you should go back to Affordability Guideline #2, which states that your monthly housing expenses (mortgage, property taxes, homeowner's insurance and association fees, if applicable) should be no more than 25% of your monthly gross income, and use these computations to see if you can afford the home. Now that you have a ballpark figure on how much you can afford, start looking. Many students like to do this stage entirely on the internet, although this also can be done by talking to a real estate agent. If you do decide to talk to an agent or a broker, keep some courtesies in mind:

1. Let them know that you are working on a project for a class you are taking and not actually in the market for a house. Most agents are paid through commissions. For this reason and others some people may not want to spend time with you. Others will gladly help you out. From their perspective, it is always good to build good will. Besides, if they are helpful, you may remember their name and go back to them when

you are ready to buy a home. But remember, be up front with them so that they can decide if they want to help you or not.

2. If you do decide to talk to an agent, choose a time when their offices are not busy. Morning and mid-afternoon are probably good times. Lunch hours and weekends are probably not good times.

For this assignment you need to hand in the following:

1. Restate the amount of money you plan to save over the 5 year period. Assuming that this amount is the 20% down payment, what is the total cost of the house you can buy?

2. Restate your projected salary. Assuming you buy a house that does not cost more than 3 times your annual gross salary, what is the maximum total cost of the house you can buy?

3. If you have saved more than 20% of the amount you found in #2, you can look for a house that costs a bit more than what you found in #2. If you have saved less than 20%, then you will have to look for a cheaper house. If you have saved more than 20%, it is OK to just go with the amount in #2. Remember there will be closing costs (you will find these in mini-project 5) and it would be nice to have some money left in your savings account. You will probably want to buy some furniture when you move in!

4. Attach a print out of the Multiple Listing Service (MLS) for your new home. Also remember it does not have to be a house, it can be a condominium or a town house. If there are no houses or condominiums listed in your price range, attach the MLS print out for the closest listing you found. It is important to note at this point: you are not being graded on this project according to your ability to buy a home. Many of you will find that it is not realistic financially to be buying a home 5 years after graduation. That is fine. The point of the project is to research the process of buying a home, not actually buy a house.

Mini-project 5:

Now you need to take out a loan to buy the house. In today's market there are many loan options. For the purpose of this project, however, we will restrict our research to a fixed or adjustable rate mortgage. First, you need to decide whether you want to go with a fixed or adjustable mortgage and whether you want to loan for 15 or 30 years (or maybe 20). Any bank or mortgage lender website should have information on the different interest rate amounts for fixed or adjustable rates and different loan durations. Again you can talk to a banking professional but remember the courtesies stated above. You should describe the different types of mortgages, make a decision as to what type of mortgage you would get, and explain why in this assignment.

The next thing you should do is research all the closing costs associated with taking out a loan to buy a house. These closing costs include origination fees, discount fees, appraisal fees, and many other fees. It is your responsibility in this assignment to find out all the pertinent fees and to explain what they mean. So you should include an itemized list of all closing costs which will include a short description of what each of these costs mean. Sometimes a bank will offer a special where they waive closing costs to get your business. If you find a lender who is doing this, this does not excuse you from doing the research required in this assignment. Remember the point of this project is to learn about the process of buying a home. Once you have ascertained all closing costs, remember these are costs that need to be paid on the day that you purchase the home. Therefore, these costs must be deducted from the money that you have saved towards a down payment.

 At this point you should be able to list all your monthly housing costs. These costs will include the mortgage payment (show the computations), the property taxes (these are often listed on the MLS for the home), homeowner's insurance (again you will probably need to talk to an agent), private mortgage insurance (if your down payment is less than 20% of the price of the home, you will need to pay this insurance to the lender to protect the lender against the higher likelihood of foreclosure). The private mortgage insurance is typically 0.5% of the price of the home. Some of you will also have to pay a homeowner's association fees (typically charged to all owners of condominiums and townhouses and often charged to single dwelling homeowners that live in a subdivision. Again, this fee is generally stated in the house's listing that you included with mini-project 4). Once you have come up with the total of these monthly housing costs, you should check to see that they are no more than 25% of your projected monthly income (Affordability guideline #2).

FINAL REPORT: This portion must be word processed

Now is the time to write you final report. The point of the mini-assignments was to research the specifics of the process of buying a home. You will get little credit for this assignment, however, if all you do is submit the mini-assignments. Use the information you compiled in the mini-projects to write a cohesive, coherent, and professional paper about buying a house. All the information that was included in your mini-projects should be included in this paper. Do not assume that I remember the information from the mini-projects. Remember, any good paper has an introduction and a conclusion. All computations should be shown. Even though most mortgage lenders include a calculator on their websites that will calculate your monthly principal and interest payments, you need to show the computations using the formula from the textbook.

Your project must include:

1. Title page
2. Table of contents.
3. Introduction (discussing the goal of the project).
4. Body (information from all portions of the mini-assignments 1-5).
5. All formulas used for calculations. These may be word processed or written in ink. They must be in the correct format.
6. Conclusion (summarize the important points about your salary, home and loan).
7. The Multiple Listing Service (MLS) picture of your home.
8. List of formulas used in your project. These formulas must include the name of the formula, the formula written in proper form, a definition of all variables, and a brief description of what the formula tells you.
9. List of all references. This should include any banks, realtors, insurance agents, and websites. If you talked to any people, you should give their names and their employer.

Your report must be word processed. The text of your paper should be 5-10 pages (this does not include the formulas). It should be free of errors in spelling and grammar. It will be graded for a demonstrated understanding of the project, completeness, organization, following instructions, and professional formatting.

Grading Percentages

In general my grading percentages are as follows:

Mathematics – 40%. The points here are awarded for coming up with accurate numbers throughout the project. The point of the mini-projects is for you to send me the research that you have done so I can check your mathematical accuracy and comment on your research.

Explanations – 40%. These points are awarded according to how well you explain all your computations and the research you have done.

Style – 20%. This is my rather subjective category that covers the quality of the writing and organization of your paper.

PROFESSIONAL BIBLIOGRAPHY

Books and Journal Articles

Aldrich, Vickie, Elaine Cohen, and Lynne Hartsell. *Collaborative Learning Manual*. Reading MA: Addison-Wesley, 1994.

Angelo, Thomas A, and K. Patricia Cross. *Classroom Assessment Techniques: A Handbook for College Teachers*, 2nd ed. San Francisco: Jossey-Bass, 1993.

Arem, Cynthia. *Conquering Math Anxiety: A Self-Help Workbook* (with CD-ROM). Belmont, CA: Brooks/Cole, 2002.

Bennett, Jeffrey O. and William L. Briggs. *Using and Understanding Mathematics: A Quantitative Reasoning Approach*, 2nd ed. Boston: Addison-Wesley, 2002.

Boyer, Carl B. A *History of Mathematics*, 2nd ed. Revised by Uta C. Merzbach. New York: John Wiley and Sons, 1991.

Charles, C. M. *Essentials of Effective Discipline*. Boston: Allyn & Bacon, 2002.

Gardner, Howard. *Multiple Intelligences: The Theory in Practice*. New York: Basic Books, 1993.

Gregg, Diana Underwood and Erna Yackel. "Helping Students Make Sense of Algebraic Expressions: The Candy Shop." *Mathematics Teaching in the Middle School* 7, no. 9 (2002): 492.

Greive, Donald (Ed.). *A Handbook for Adjunct and Part-time Faculty and Teachers of Adults*. 4th ed. Elyria, Ohio: Info-Tec, 2003.

Greive, Donald and Catherine Worden (Eds.). *Handbook II; Advanced Teaching Strategies for Adjunct Faculty*. Ann Arbor: Adjunct Advocate, Inc., 2000.

Hagelgans, N. et al. *A Practical Guide to Cooperative Learning in Collegiate Mathematics*. Notes Number 37. Washington, D.C.: The Mathematical Association of America, 1995.

Jensen, Eric. *The Learning Brain*. San Diego: Turning Point Publishing, 1994.

Johnson, David W., Roger T. Johnson, and Kurt Smith. *Active Learning: Cooperation in the College Classroom*. Edina, MN: Interaction Book Company, 1998.

Johnson, David W. and Roger T. Johnson. *Meaningful Assessment: A Manageable and Cooperative Process*. Boston: Allyn & Bacon, 2002.

Johnson, Mildred. *How to Solve Word Problems in Algebra*. Columbus, OH: McGraw-Hill, 1992.

Jones, Vernon F. and Louise S. Jones. *Comprehensive Classroom Management: Creating Communities of Support and Solving Problems*, 6th ed. Boston: Allyn & Bacon, 2002.

Journal of Developmental Education

Kitchens, Anita Narvarte. *Defeating Math Anxiety*. Chicago: Richard D. Irwin, Inc., 1995.

Marcy, Steve and Janis Marcy. *Algebra with Pizzazz!* Creative Publications, 1996.

Mathematical Association of America, Committee on the Teaching of Undergraduate Mathematics. *College Mathematics: Suggestions on How to Teach It.* Washington, D.C.: The Mathematical Association of America, 1979.

McKeachie, Wilbert J. and Barbara K. Hofer (Eds.) *McKeachie's Teaching Strategies, Research, and Theory*, 11th ed. Boston: Houghton Mifflin Company, 2002.

Nahin, Paul J. *An Imaginary Tale: The Story of* . Princeton: Princeton University Press, 1998.

Nolting, Paul. *Winning at Math*. Bradenton, FL: Academic Success Press, Inc., 1991.

Ooten, Cheryl. *Managing the Mean Math Blues*. Upper Saddle River, NJ: Prentice Hall, 2003.

Pappas, Theoni. *The Joy of Mathematics*. San Carlos, CA: Wide World Publishing, 1989.

———— *More Joy of Mathematics*. San Carlos, CA: Wide World Publishing, 1991.

Paulos, John Allen. *Innumeracy: Mathematical Illiteracy and Its Consequences*. New York: Farrar, Straus and Girous, 1989.

Peterson, Ivars. *The Mathematical Tourist: New and Updated Snapshots of Modern Mathematics*. New York: W. H. Freeman, 1998.

Popham, W. James. *Classroom Assessment: What Teachers Need to Know*, 3rd ed. Boston: Allyn & Bacon, 2002.

Schwartzman, Steven. *The Words of Mathematics: An Etymological Dictionary of Mathematical Terms Used in English*. Washington, D.C.: The Mathematical Association of America, 1994.

Science News magazine

Smith, Sanderson. *Agnesi to Zeno: Over 100 Vignettes from the History of Math*. Emeryville, CA: Key Curriculum Press, 1996.

Sterrett, Andrew. *Using Writing to Teach Mathematics* (MAA Math Note 16). Washington: The Mathematical Association of America, 1992.

Sutton, Suzanne. "Remedies for the Pain of Math Anxiety." *ENC Focus Review*. Washington, D.C.: U.S. Department of Education Eisenhower National Clearinghouse (May 2004).

Special thanks to Olivia Garcia of The University of Texas at Brownsville and Texas Southmost College for contributing the following Mathematics Education bibliography.

American Mathematical Association of Two-Year Colleges. *Crossroads in Mathematics: Standards for Introductory College Mathematics before Calculus.* Memphis, TN: AMATYC, 1995.

Applefield, J. M., R. Huber, and M. Moallem. "Constructivism in Theory and Practice: Toward a Better Understanding." *The High School Journal* 84, no. 2 (2000): 35–53.

Boyd, P. C. and S. B. Cooper. "Communication in the Mathematics Classroom." *Kappa Delta Record* 34, no. 3 (1998): 102–105.

Campbell, L., B. Campbell, and D. Dickinson. *Teaching and Learning through Multiple Intelligences.* Needham Heights, MA: Allyn & Bacon, 1996.

Carlson, M. P. "Obstacles for College Algebra Students in Understanding Functions: What do High-performing Students Really Know?" *AMATYC Review* 19, no. 1 (1997): 48–59.

Cowen, C. C. "Teaching and Testing Mathematics Reading." *American Mathematical Monthly* 98, no. 1 (1991): 50–53.

Davidson, N. *Cooperative Learning in Mathematics: A Handbook for Teachers.* Menlo Park, CA: Addison-Wesley, 1990.

Davidson, R. and E. Levitov. *Overcoming Math Anxiety,* 2nd ed. New York: HarperCollins College Publishers, 1993.

Durkin, K. "Language in mathematical education: An introduction." In K. Durkin & B. Shire (Eds.). *Language in mathematical education: Research and practices.* Bristol, PA: Open University Press, 1991: 3–16.

Edwards, H. C. "Mistakes and Other Classroom Techniques: An Application of Social Learning Theory." *Journal on Excellence in College Teaching*, 4 (1993): 49–60.

Esty, W. W. "Language Concepts of Mathematics." *Focus on Learning Problems in Mathematics* 14, no. 4 (1992): 31–54.

———— *The Language of Mathematics.* Unpublished manuscript, Department of Mathematical Sciences, Montana State University-Bozeman, 1997.

Esty, W. W. and A. R. Teppo. "A General-Education Course Emphasizing Mathematical Language and Reasoning." *Focus on Learning Problems in Mathematics* 16, no. 1 (1994): 13–35.

Faust, J. L. and D.R. Paulson. (1998). "Active Learning in the College Classroom." *Journal on Excellence in College Teaching* 9, no. 2 (1998), 3–24.

Gardner, H. *Frames of Mind: The Theory of Multiple Intelligences.* New York: Basic Books, Inc., 1983.

Green, T. D. "Responding and Sharing: Techniques for Energizing Classroom Discussions." *The Clearing House* 73, no. 6 (2000): 331–334.

Haladyna, T. *Writing Test Items to Evaluate Higher Order Thinking.* Boston: Allyn & Bacon, 1997.

Hart, L. C. "The Status of Research on Postsecondary Mathematics Education." *Journal on Excellence in College Teaching* 10, no. 2 (1999): 3–26.

Kaur, B. and B.H.P. Sharon. "Algebraic Misconceptions of First Year College Students." *Focus on Learning Problems in Mathematics* 16, no. 4 (1994): 43–58.

Kenney, P. A., C.G. Schloemer, and R.W. Cain. "Communicating about Alternative Assessment beyond the Mathematics Classroom. In P. C. Elliot and M. J. Kenney (Eds.). *Communication in Mathematics K–12 and Beyond* (1996 Yearbook). Reston, VA: National Council of Teachers of Mathematics, 1996: 187–196.

Meier, J. and T. Rishel. *Writing in the Teaching and Learning of Mathematics.* MAA Notes Number 48. Washington, DC: The Mathematical Association of America, 1998.

Miller, C.A. and B.D. Smith. "Assessment of Prerequisite Mathematics Vocabulary Terms for Intermediate and College Algebra." *Focus on Learning Problems in Mathematics* 16, no.2 (1994): 39–50.

Munroe, E. E. and R. Panchyshyn. "Vocabulary Considerations for Teaching Mathematics." *Childhood Education* 72, no. 2 (1995): 80–83.

National Council of Teachers of Mathematics. *Curriculum and Evaluation Standards for School Mathematics.* Reston, VA: NCTM, 1989.

———— *Professional Standards for Teaching Mathematics.* Reston, VA: NCTM, 1991.

———— *Mathematics Assessment: Myths, Models, Good Questions, and Practical Suggestions.* Reston, VA: NCTM, 1991.

———— *Connecting Mathematics Across the Curriculum.* Reston, VA: NCTM, 1995.

———— *Communication in Mathematics K–12 and Beyond.* Reston, VA: NCTM, 1996.

———— *Principles and Standards for School Mathematics.* Reston, VA: NCTM, 2000.

Nelan, C. "Conquer the Gap in Mathematics." *College Teaching* 45 (1997): 82.

Pimm, D. "Communicating Mathematically." In K. Durkin and B. Shire (Eds.). *Language in Mathematical Education: Research and Practices.* Bristol, PA: Open University Press, 1991: 17–23.

Rubenstein, R. N. and Thompson, D. R. "Learning Mathematical Symbolism: Challenges and Instructional Strategies". *Mathematics Teacher* 94, no. 4 (2001): 265–271.

Sembra, A. and Hovis, M. "*Math a Four Letter Word: The Math Anxiety Handbook.*" Wimberly, TX: The Wimberly Press, 1996.

Thompson, D. R. and R. N. Rubenstein. "Learning Mathematics Vocabulary: Potential Pitfalls and Instructional Strategies." *Mathematics Teacher* 93, no. 7 (2000): 568–574.

Usiskin, Z. "Mathematics as a Language." In P.C. Elliott & M. J. Kenney (Eds.). *Communicating in Mathematics, K–12 and Beyond* (1996 Yearbook). Reston, VA: National Council of Teachers of Mathematics, 1996: 231–243.

Winston, R.B. Jr., W.C. Bonney, T.K. Miller, and J.C. Dagley. *Promoting Student Development through Intentionally Structured Groups.* San Francisco, CA: Jossey-Bass, 1988.

Zepp, R. *Language and Mathematics Education.* Publication for Teachers and Practitioners, Hong Kong. (ERIC Reproduction Service No. ED 312 143), 1989.

Web Links

www.aaamath.com

www.algebrahelp.com

www.amatyc.org   American Mathematical Association of Two-Year Colleges

www.ams.org   American Mathematical Society

www.analyzemath.com   Mathematics tutorials and applications

www.aw.com/aw/events   Addison-Wesley Conference and Workshop Site

www.census.gov   U.S. Census Bureau (excellent source for real data)

www.coolmath.com

www.co-operation.org   The Cooperative Learning Center at the University of Minnesota

www.dyscalculia.org/DIC.html   Dyscalculia International Consortium

www.gap-system.org/~history   The MacTutor History of Mathematics archive

www.hawaii.edu/suremath/home.html   21st Century Problem Solving

www.ies.co.jp/math   International Education Software

www.imacc.org/standards/   Crossroads in Mathematics: *Standards for Teaching College Mathematics Before Calculus*

www.maa.org   Mathematical Association of America

www.maa.org/cupm   Committee on the Undergraduate Curriculum in Mathematics

www.mathematicshelpcentral.com

www.mathforum.org/math.topics.html   The Math Forum at Drexel University

www.mathnotes.com/aw_span_gloss.html   Spanish Glossary

www.mathpower.com

www.mathworld.wolfram.com

www.merlot.com   Multimedia Educational Resource for Learning and Online Teaching

www.nctm.org   The National Council of Teachers of Mathematics

www.purplemath.com

www.quickmath.com   QuickMath Automatic Math Solutions

www.sosmath.com   S.O.S. Mathematics

www.thinkquest.com/library/index.html   ThinkQuest Library

www.umkc.edu/cad/made   National Association for Developmental Education